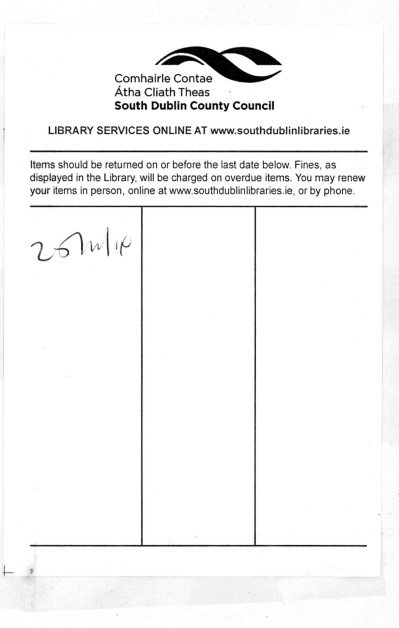

Comhairle Contae
Átha Cliath Theas
South Dublin County Council

LIBRARY SERVICES ONLINE AT www.southdublinlibraries.ie

Items should be returned on or before the last date below. Fines, as
displayed in the Library, will be charged on overdue items. You may renew
your items in person, online at www.southdublinlibraries.ie, or by phone.

26/11/16

Also by John Adair

Effective Communication
Effective Decision Making
Effective Innovation
Effective Leadership
Effective Leadership Masterclass
Effective Motivation
Effective Strategic Leadership
Effective Teambuilding
Effective Time Management

CONFUCIUS
ON
LEADERSHIP

JOHN ADAIR

MACMILLAN

First published 2013 by Macmillan
an imprint of Pan Macmillan, a division of Macmillan Publishers Limited
Pan Macmillan, 20 New Wharf Road, London N1 9RR
Basingstoke and Oxford
Associated companies throughout the world
www.panmacmillan.com

ISBN 978-1-4472-1880-7

1 3 5 7 9 8 6 4 2

A CIP catalogue record for this book is available from
the British Library.

Typeset by SetSystems Ltd, Saffron Walden, Essex
Printed and bound by CPI Group (UK) Ltd, Croydon, CR0 4YY

Visit **www.panmacmillan.com** to read more about all our books
and to buy them. You will also find features, author interviews and
news of any author events, and you can sign up for e-newsletters
so that you're always first to hear about our new releases.

CONTENTS

AUTHOR'S NOTE

As far as we know, Confucius himself wrote no books, but his disciples made a collection of his sayings. Known in English as the *Analects*, from a Greek word meaning fragments left over after a meal, this anthology is our principal source for his teaching.

The *Analects* also contain some personal glimpses of Confucius the man, caught in amber for all time. I hope they may serve to bring him to life for you as an alternative and engaging person in the following pages.

For reference purposes, the *Analects* is divided into chapters and verses, not unlike the books of the Bible or the Qur'an. There are some slight variations between different translations of the *Analects* in English; the references in this book follow the system in the Penguin Classics edition (1979).

References to chapter and verse in the *Tao-te-Ching* (The Book of the Way and its Power) attributed to Lao-tzu also follow the Penguin Classics edition (1963).

INTRODUCTION

Welcome to this book. In its pages you will find an opportunity to explore for yourself the practical wisdom of ancient China on the theme of leadership. The intention of both Confucius and myself is that by so doing you will take some significant steps towards your aim of becoming the best leader it lies within you to be.

Until you picked up this book Confucius may have been no more than a name to you, so let me briefly introduce him here and explain why he has so much to offer you. If you would like to refresh your mind about his life and times, I suggest you turn to my brief biography of him in the Appendix.

Confucius is the Latinized form of his Chinese name. That was composed of three elements: *Kung*, the family name; *fu*, a title of respect or honour not unlike 'mister' in English; and *tzu*, (*zi*) a title of honour which means 'Master'. Thanks to a modern transliteration system, the Chinese today refer to him as *Kung-Zi*. You will notice that his disciples or students called him simply 'The Master'. And in Chinese culture he is indeed considered a Master of Masters.

1

If you look up Confucius in the reference books, you will find that he is usually classified as a philosopher. This is correct, but he is not a philosopher in the Western analytical sense. Like his near contemporary Socrates, he is really a practical philosopher. And his principal concern was to apply his clear thinking and learning to the immense task he took upon his own shoulders: to ensure that in the future China would have good leaders and leaders for good.

And so Confucius was the world's first great teacher of leadership. That, I know, is a bold claim; I shall have to wait until you have read the book to see if you accept it as true.

It is only very recently that we have been able to appreciate the contributions of these two great teachers of leadership – Confucius in the East and Socrates in the West. What has made it easier to do so is my work (as yet unfinished) of assembling together for the first time the world's universal body of knowledge about leadership and leadership development. And that has been made possible by a great discovery in the context of this field, namely the identification at last of the generic role of *leader* (see Chapter 1). It is in the light of that breakthrough that you will best be able to assess the value of what Confucius has to offer on this subject.

A moment ago I mentioned the word *role*. Originally, role meant the part taken by an actor in a play. In our wider usage it now refers to a person's characteristic or expected function. According to a common saying, it is the expectations of people that determine a person's particular role in a human group or society. Note also a phrase introduced relatively recently into the English language: *role model* – a person who is regarded by others as an outstandingly good example of a particular role.

It follows that your first step on the road to excellence as a leader is to be clear what the generic role of *leader* is, so that you will know what your people will be expecting from you. That is roughly what Confucius was attempting to teach the princes and government leaders of his day. But thanks to the fact that the role of leader is generic, you can translate his wisdom to apply to your present responsibility as a business leader. Do you see what I mean?

That process, of course, is going to call for active participation on your part. Great teachers are also great leaders, and Confucius strikes an authentic note as a leader when he makes demands on us to play our full part in the creation of practical wisdom.

> The Master said, 'I never enlighten anyone who has not been driven to distraction by trying to understand a difficulty or who has not got into a frenzy trying to put his ideas into words. When I have pointed out one corner of a square to anyone and he does not come back with the other three, I will not point it out to him a second time.'
>
> *Analects*, 11:8

What I like about this saying is that it is an invitation to you and me to exercise our creativity: to build on ideas, explore possibilities and to make connections that Confucius himself – remember that he lived 2,500 years ago – could hardly have even dreamt of making. In this respect we are challenged to emulate Tzu-kung, one of his closest disciples, of whom Confucius said: 'Tell such a man something and he can see its relevance to what he has not been told' (*Analects*, 1:15).

So you and I together have to complete the squares and triangles that Confucius begins with a single thought. Are you up for the challenge?

If you respond to Confucius' thought leadership in the way that Tzu-kung did in his day, I am completely confident that by the end of reading and reflecting on this book you will have in your keeping:

- ☙ a clear vision of the generic role of *leader* – what you need to be, to know and to do.

- ☙ the encouragement to apply those principles in your day-to-day work as a leader.

- ☙ a deeper understanding of human nature and what people expect of their leader.

- ☙ the opportunity to review, confirm or amend your own set of values as a leader.

- ☙ a firm grasp of the global body of knowledge concerning leadership and leadership development

– the basis of effective leadership in any
international context.

Apart from these personal benefits, I believe this book
is important for a global reason. Now that China is assuming such a dominant role among the nations of the world,
the big question is this: will China adopt the somewhat
flawed Western models of hegemony, or will it be true to
its own moral tradition – the tradition that begins with
Confucius and which I outline for you in this book?

To end on a personal note, in 2005 the People's
Republic of China kindly appointed me their Honorary
Professor of Leadership, making me the first non-Chinese
person in history to be offered the mantle of Confucius. It
is an honour I cherish, and this book is but a small token
of my thanks.

PART ONE

THE GENERIC ROLE
OF LEADER

1

WHAT IS LEADERSHIP?

'Listen to all, pluck a feather from every passing
goose, but follow no one absolutely.'
Chinese proverb

For Confucius, clear thinking and good leadership go hand
in hand. And central to clear thinking, he believes, is what
he called the right use of names – the words we use to
denote objects of thought, such as the words by which a
person, animal, place or thing is known, spoken of or
addressed. Confucius, however, doesn't advocate a striving
for precision for its own sake. What he is after is clarity of
expression, not a scrupulous precision. 'It is enough', he
says, 'that the language one uses gets the point across'
(15:41). He is essentially a practical thinker.

> Tzu-lu said, 'If the Lord of Wei left the administration
> [*cheng*] of his state to you, what would you put first?'
> The Master said, 'If something has to be put first,
> it is, perhaps, the rectification [*cheng*] of names.' [The

two uses of *cheng* in Chinese are distinguished only by intonation.]

Tzu-lu said, 'Is that so? What a roundabout way you take! Why bring rectification in at all?'

The Master said, 'When names are not correct, what is said will not sound reasonable; when what is said does not sound reasonable, affairs will not culminate in success ... Thus when the gentleman names something, the name is sure to be usable in speech, and when he says something this is sure to be practicable. The thing about the gentleman is that he is anything but casual where speech is concerned.'* (13:3)

Following this guidance from the Master, we need to be clear from the outset what the names *leader*, *leading* and *leadership* mean in English. As we shall see, failure to undertake this initial step has led to much confusion among many contemporary writers on the subject of leadership – especially in the United States, the world's greatest publisher of such books.

As far as I know, these English names had no equivalent in Chinese as spoken and written 2,500 years ago. In modern Chinese there are words used for *leader* and *leadership*, but the images behind them do not tie up with

---

* With this may be compared the words given to Socrates by Plato in *Phaedo:* 'You may be sure, dear Crito, that inaccurate language is not only in itself a mistake; it implants evil in men's souls.'

10

those that give their English counterparts their distinctive and recognizable meaning.

Languages do, of course, borrow words from each other. The vast majority of English words borrowed from Chinese are ordinary loan words with regular phonetic adaptation, such as *chop suey* (Cantonese *tsap-sui*, meaning miscellaneous pieces). But *losing face*, a phrase so firmly established in the English vocabulary that the average Englishman is totally unaware of its Chinese origin, is more than such an ordinary loan: it fills a real gap in the English language, just as does the borrowed French word *morale*.

In the last two or three decades, other languages, which – like Chinese – have no native equivalent to the English word of *leader*, have done the obvious thing. French, Spanish, Polish, Finnish and Japanese, for example, have invisibly imported *leader* into their own lexicons.

Although Confucius didn't have a name for it, he certainly had a concept of a general role in human affairs concerned with direction, one that was distinct from the more specialized roles, functions, trades or professions occupied by the larger majority of men.

Confucius relates this nameless generalist role to being 'a gentleman'. When he wasn't engaged in study or thought (the other acceptable occupations), a gentleman contributed to society in this way.

The Chinese name *junzi*, which is usually translated

11

into English as gentleman, originally referred to the son of a ruler (*jun* meaning ruler; *zi* meaning son), and therefore one destined to be a man in authority. *Jun* originally referred to an ancient state sovereign, the governor or ruler. Traditionally, the firstborn son of such a ruler would be educated and cultivated according to the highest standard of knowledge and ethics. So they were often the moral models for others. The word *junzi* therefore came to be used for those people who have honourable traits and achievements, civilized men of high moral principle.

Later on, *junzi* came to have even wider meanings, such as a good person or a good husband. By the day of Confucius, the word gentleman – much as in English – had come to be used in a wider cultural sense, signifying a civilized and moral man. Yet it had quite lost its connotation of a person who could be regarded as set above others by personal qualities, one who is thus fit to lead and model the best behaviour to others.

Apart from rulers and their sons, in ancient China there was a class of men who constituted what in England would be called the gentry. Usually they came from families who had acquired the dignity of having surnames – Confucius came from the Kung family – and they were eligible for office in the higher administrative or military hierarchies of their states. Taken as a whole, Confucius argued, their function is to contribute to the direction and control of society. As the picture begins to emerge from the *Analects* of that generalist role – what you have to do and what you have to be – it is clear that Confucius is really talking about leadership as we know it today. Hence this book.

In ancient China, a highly specific role in society – or the person who performed it – was known as a vessel. It is a metaphor the Chinese drew from everyday life: a vessel is a hollow receptacle designed to hold liquid, such as a cask, cup, pot, bottle or dish; in other words, it tends to have a self-evidently specialized function. Vessels used in sacrificial rites in temples were commonly made of jade, a hard stone usually green in colour:

> Tzu-kung asked, 'What do you think of me?'
> The Master said, 'You are a vessel.'
> 'What kind of vessel?'
> 'A sacrificial vessel.' (5:4)

Incidentally, the obvious interpretation here, that Confucius judged Tzu-kung to be suited by interest, aptitude and temperament to become a priest in one of the great state temples, cannot be correct. For we know that Tzu-kung, whom we have already met in the Introduction, did not become a priest. In fact, he was the only one of the three best-known disciples of Confucius to survive their Master. He went on to have a distinguished career as a diplomat and a merchant. By calling him 'a sacrificial vessel' here, I think that Confucius probably meant that Tzu-kung

– like himself – had been called by Heaven (or as if by Heaven) to be what William Wordsworth called 'a dedicated spirit', a man set aside for a high purpose or special destiny.

The leader or gentleman is not a vessel in the sense of being limited to a highly specialized function, as Confucius makes clear (2:12). Interestingly enough, however, even in those days men tended to be highly esteemed only if they had some specialist knowledge or skill, like a master builder or musician. Such proficiency granted them a local reputation, if not fame, in their own profession, and without it they were hardly rated by their neighbours. When one of Confucius' neighbours drew attention to his lack of this sort of reputation, the Master replied with some humour:

> A man from a village in Ta Hsiang said, 'Great indeed is Confucius! He has wide learning but has not made a name for himself in any field.' The Master, on hearing of this, said to his disciples, 'What should I make myself proficient in? In driving? Or in archery? I think I would prefer driving.' (9:2)

Confucius, it seems, was a practical man when it came to the kind of menial work that servants do around the house or on the land. He had acquired these skills, he once explained to Tzu-kung, because: 'I was of humble station when young'. But that was a mere accident in his case; he did not expect all gentlemen to possess the same competencies. 'Should a gentleman be skilled in many things? No, not at all' (9:9). He himself had 'never been proved in office' – that is, he had never made his name as a specialist in government: 'That is why I am not an expert in any one field' (9:7).

The distinctive use of the word vessel to mean a specialist is also found in the *Tao-te-Ching* (The Book of the Way and its Power), the central Taoist text ascribed to Lao-tzu, the traditional founder of Taoism. Thought to have been originally written as a guide for rulers on how to be a sage – Lao's term for a truly excellent leader – it serves as the classic introduction to the *Tao* (the Way), a concept shared widely by Chinese thinkers, including Confucius, in China at that time.

There is some doubt if the Master *Lao* (meaning old man) ever really existed as an individual person, as opposed to being the personalized name of a tradition. Either way, it is clear that Confucius had much in common with Lao-tzu. Hence there is at least some poetic truth in the ancient legend that in his younger days he once made a long journey to meet Lao-tzu and received instruction from him, apparently in the proper conduct of rituals.

Lao-tzu argues that in contrast to vessels – specific work functions that have names, like individual trades and crafts – the role of the ruler is innominate, or nameless. He compares it to a block of uncarved jade hewn from a quarry that also lacks a name.

Likewise, the Way itself – which the sage both follows and exemplifies – is also nameless. For a name in Taoist thought is always the name of a specific thing; it distinguishes one thing from another. But the Way has no limits or boundaries. Therefore to give the Way a name – or set of names – would run the risk of restricting it at the level of unconscious assumptions as to one function or kind of work rather than another. Like the wind, the Way is no respecter of definitions or boundaries. Nor does it have the self-consciousness that comes with having a name, not to mention a reputation.

As we have seen, it is specialist expertise in named functions that tends to bring honour, fame and glory upon a man's head. Therefore the Way – lacking a name – is essentially humble. Like water, it always falls to the lowest level where it comes to rest. In relation to the myriad creatures

> It gives them life yet claims no possession;
> It benefits them yet exacts no gratitude;
> It is the steward yet exercises no authority. (51:116)

The sage, occupying a generalist role that has no name and reliant on the nameless Way, is presented as being entirely self-effacing in relation to his people. In particular, he makes no claim upon them for any reciprocal kind of reward or recognition. He gives freely and constantly, yet expects no reward – not even the reward of being noticed:

> The sage benefits them yet exacts no gratitude,
> Accomplishes his task yet lays claim to no merit.
>   (77:185)

Therefore, like the rough block of marble with no name and thus no cause for pride, the truly excellent leader exemplifies humility. Humility derives from a Latin word which has as its basis *humus* – the earth. The Old English equivalent was lowliness: thus Jesus describes himself in the English Bible as being 'lowly in spirit', that is, without self-pride or haughtiness. Perhaps in this context self-effacing is a better term. A justly famous expression of this inner spirit of lowliness comes in Chapter 17 of the *Tao-te-Ching*:

> The best of all rulers is but a shadowy presence to
>   his subjects.
> Next best is the ruler they love and praise;
> Next comes one they fear;
> Next comes one with whom they [despise or] take
>   liberties with.
> Fail to respect and trust people, they will fail to show
>   respect and trust.
> [The great ruler] talks but little.
> When his task is accomplished and his work done
> The people all say, 'It happened to us naturally.'

That same spirit – the willingness to put one's ego into the background – is still a hallmark of excellence. It doesn't spring, however, from the fact that one's generalist role lacks a name, as Lao-tzu and Confucius believed. For in English that universal role does have a name: *leadership*.

In Old English the noun *lead* meant a path, way, road or course (as of a ship at sea). It is by origin a journey word. Thus to lead means to show others the way, especially by going out in front. A *leader* is the agent or doer that does the leading.

Incidentally, the verb in Old English is in the causative form, so it means to cause or make others to go on a journey. But the assumption hidden in the word *leading* is always that others will be following freely or willingly, of their own accord. There is no hint of the use of force to compel others to move against their will. Once you get out a gun and threaten people to make them go with you, you have stepped out of the domain of leadership.

Indeed, it is as if the very fact of the leader going ahead and showing the way is enough to make the others follow. It is probably the case that for humans, being social beings, the instinct to follow a leader in the literal sense is buried deep within our genes. Vestigial as it may be, here we share something in common with all living creatures that flock together and like to move as one body. As the Chinese proverb says,

> Not the cry but the flight of the wild duck,
> Leads the flock to fly and to follow.

Usually at the level of people – groupings of persons – there is more to it than simply animal instinct. We are more complicated than sheep. A leader in human society is one who is voluntarily followed because others perceive in him or her an ability to lead the way forward in that particular context or situation. Thus *leadership* in its first sense means just that. For the suffix *-ship* in English – as in words like craftsmanship or horsemanship – indicates the presence of ability or skill.

But the suffix *-ship* is ambiguous – hence the reason why so many American writers have been confused by the word *leadership*. For it can also mean a position, office or status, as it does in chairmanship or dealership. In this second sense, *leadership* refers merely to those who happen to be occupying positions as heads of groups or organizations, communities or nations. Thus we talk in this generic way about the leadership of a particular industry or trades union, or the leadership of a particular political party. Whether or not those we so refer to in this kind of general use actually demonstrate leadership in the first sense – the ability to lead – is, of course, an entirely different question.

In fact, it is arguably more often the case than not that those who are leaders in the second sense – holders of leadership positions – lack the quality of leadership in the first sense. Plutarch, the Greek writer of the second century CE, described the unfortunate Roman politician Gaius Antonius, elected to the highest office in Rome, as 'a man with no aptitude for leadership in any direction, either good or bad'. And it was said of the Roman emperor Galba that everyone thought he would make a great emperor until he actually occupied the office.

Confucius observed the same phenomenon in his own time and place, which suggests that it is a universal problem:

'What about men who are in public life in the present day?'

The Master said, 'Oh, they are of such limited capacity that they hardly count.' (19.20)

Does this mismatch between holders of the office of leadership and leadership ability matter? Clearly Confucius thought that it did. Otherwise why would he go to such lengths to sow the seeds of a new kind of leadership in China, providing advice for the sages of tomorrow?

Does it matter today? Of course it does. More so, in fact, because the consequences of the lack of leadership in public life – in politics and business life, not least in that form of economic management we call banking – reverberate throughout the world. In our complex and interdependent world, vulnerable to disruption, few things are more important than the quality and credibility of leaders.

In all cultures and languages, positions of leadership in fields such as military, business or sport have specific names, and their responsibilities are usually well known. One metaphorical term that we use for them – not exclusively, of course – is *roles*.

English borrowed the word role from the old French, where it reflected a metaphor drawn from the theatre. The roll of paper upon which an actor's part was written became in time the part itself, and then, by a further extension, a person's characteristic or expected function in life.

The key word here is expected. For it is a set of social expectations that more or less defines a person's role. For example, we expect waiters, policemen or doctors to behave in certain ways, and these expectations clarify their roles. Such expectations attach to and help to define all the highly specific roles of leadership that have names – what musicians, for example, expect from a *conductor*, troops from their *commander*, or citizens from their *president*.

My principal contribution in this field has been the discovery of the generic role of *leader*, a prototypical role that underlies all the forms that leadership takes in the various fields of human enterprise. It applies as much to communities and nations as to working groups and organizations, although in these more diffuse settings it is sometimes difficult to make out its presence. As an introduction to understanding this generic role, let us look briefly at the earliest recorded leadership metaphors known to man – the model of shepherd and sheep.

The earliest surviving example of human writing – inscribed in cuneiform on a Sumerian clay tablet in Mesopotamia over 3,000 years before the birth of Confucius – reads: *Soldiers without a king are sheep without their shepherd*. It is the first example of a type of proverb – one that appears in many languages – testifying to a universal sense of need for effective leaders in any area of human enterprise. Why the need? Some clues are to be found by observing an Eastern shepherd at work.

Sheep were first domesticated long ago in the East by trading on their natural herd instinct to follow their leader – the dominant ram. The shepherd substituted himself for the ram, so to speak, and led the sheep by going ahead. Rather more effectively than the ram, he was able to lead them to distant pastures and sources of water. In desert conditions these daily journeys could sometimes cover many miles in a day. The Eastern shepherd, incidentally, made no use of dogs, except as guard dogs at night.

The shepherd would be careful to keep the flock together as a cohesive whole, for there is safety in numbers; he maintained some sort of order, especially on the move where there is a danger of stragglers. As a Russian proverb says: *Without a shepherd, sheep are not a flock.* For predators were always watching and waiting for their opportunity to try to scatter the flock in order to pick off their victims one by one. A good shepherd, people noted, is the one who is willing to lay down his life to protect his sheep from lions, leopards, wolves or hyenas.

The shepherd came to know his sheep as individuals: he could distinguish them by their faces and could call them by name so that they would come to him. He washed and cleaned their wounds and dealt with their ailments, carrying a weak lamb on his shoulder if necessary.

You can see that the *role* of shepherd – the prevailing

image of leadership in the ancient world – breaks down into three primary and overlapping functions: *task* – feeding the sheep, usually by leading them from in front on a journey to pasture; *group* – keeping them together as a whole flock; and *individual* – caring for each individual sheep or lamb. These three functional areas of activity are in fact common to all work groups and organizations – organizations are simply larger and more complicated work groups.

Work groups are more than the sum of their parts – they have a life of their own. If a group stays together for a certain period of time, it begins to develop a group personality, distinguishing it from all other groups, even within the same organization or field. In the latter case, this distinctiveness is sometimes called the corporate culture.

Yet, as different as you and I may be, we are both going to feel hungry and tired by the day's end: we have needs in common. There are three sets of need present in all working groups and organizations:

- the need to accomplish the common *task*;

- the need to be maintained or held together as a working and cohesive *group* or *team*;

- the need that *individuals* bring with them into the working group by virtue of being individual persons.

These sets of need are not isolated from each other in separate boxes: they are forces that are interacting constantly together for good or ill. Hence the model:

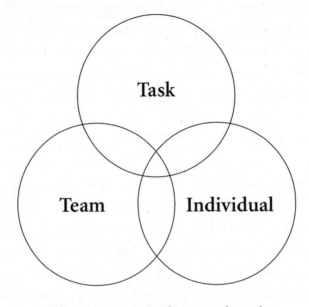

The interaction of areas of need.

You may like to explore some of the possible interactions. If, for example, you were to place a coin over the 'Task' circle, it would cover segments of the other two circles as well. In other words, lack of task or failure to achieve it will affect both team maintenance – increasing disruptive tendencies – and the area of individual needs, lowering member satisfaction within the group. Move the coin on to the 'Team' circle, and again the impact of a lack of relationships within the group on both task and individual needs may be seen at a glance.

Conversely, when a group achieves its task, the degree of group cohesiveness and enjoyment of membership should go up. Morale, both corporate and individual, will be higher. And if the members of a group happen to get on extremely well together and find that they can work closely as a team, this will increase their performance at work and also meet some important needs that individuals bring with them into common life.

Clearly, in order that the group should fulfil its task and be held together as a working team, certain *functions* will have to be performed. By function, I mean any behaviour, words or actions that meet one or more spheres of need, or areas of leadership responsibility. *Defining the aim, planning, controlling, evaluating, supporting* and *encouraging* are examples of what is meant by the word function in this context. A quality is what you *are*; a function is what you *do*. And each function can be performed with more or less skill.

The generic role of leader centres upon being the person who is responsible for these functions. That doesn't mean to say that leaders have to do everything themselves – it would not be possible for any one person to provide all the functions needed in a group.

Leadership responsibility exists on different levels. The Three Circles model shown above applies at all levels of an organization. In that respect it is a fractal: a repeated pattern in nature that can be observed on different levels in a system. But there are obvious differences in the form of leadership arising from the size and complexity of large organizations, and that leads in turn to more complex leadership functions. These are the key levels:

- *Team*: The leader of a team of some ten to twenty people with clearly specified tasks to achieve.

- *Operational*: The leader of a department of the organization, with more than one team leader under one's control. It is already a case of being a leader of leaders.

- *Strategic*: The leader of a whole organization, with a number of operational leaders under one's personal direction.

A simple recipe for organizational success is to make sure you have effective leaders occupying these roles and working together in harmony as a team. That is simple enough to say: I am not implying that it is easy either to achieve or to maintain that state of affairs under the pressures of life today.

There are in fact two basic sorts of human group: the hunting party and the family. The hunting party, tradition-ally male, works as a team; the most experienced and skilled hunter – not necessarily the oldest in the group – is usually their leader. From the hunting party and its cousin, the raiding party, sprang the first large human organization – the army – and ultimately from that, in the course of time, emerged all other forms of organization.

In the family, however, relations are not functional, but ontological, of the blood. The husband or father is traditionally head of the family. In most living creatures the head is in front as they move; it goes first and appears to lead the rest of the body – hence headship symbolizes leadership. And from the family stems the clan, tribe, a distinctive people or nation.

Nowadays, we tend to put organizations and communities into separate boxes, but this was not the practice in ancient times. The men of the tribe, for example, fought as a unit. In settled communities they worked together on common projects such as building each other's houses or on public works such as constructing fortifications.

In Confucius' day, there were no large organizations as we know them today, or even standing armies. If public works had to be done, such as the building of a temple, the ruler and his ministers became in effect the leaders of what had to be done. They could not contract it out to a construction company. When, for example, China needed to fortify its northern frontier against Mongolian invaders, it did not create a separate organization with its own board of directors. It was the people of China, unified under one ruler, who built the first great wall in *c.* 210 BCE, an extraordinary feat of construction extending some 2,400 kilometres (1,500 miles) across the borders of northern China, in most of its length wide enough to allow five horses to travel abreast between its watchtowers and forts.

Given this holistic view of society, it is not surprising that Confucius saw relations within the family – especially the relation between father and son – as the model and the foundation for leadership in the wider community. His idea of a harmonious society was a simple one: we occupy complementary roles, and happiness or well-being ensues when each of us fulfils the roles assigned to us.

> Duke Ching of Ch'i asked Confucius about government. Confucius answered, 'Let the ruler be a ruler, the subject a subject, the father a father, the son a son.' The Duke said, 'Splendid! Truly if the ruler be not a ruler, the subject not a subject, the father not a father, the son not a son, then even if there be grain, would I get to eat it?' (12:11)

What Confucius seems to be suggesting here, I think, is that if people understand their roles and act in accordance with them, there will be social harmony. Role differentiation and role performance, however, represent only one side of the coin. The other side of the coin is reached by asking ourselves the question: 'What is it that any particular ruler or subject, father or son, have in common?' The answer surely is our human nature: they are persons and so are we.

Indeed, the chief reason why the teaching of Confucius

on leadership has endured for some 2,500 years and still speaks to us today is the profound understanding of human nature that underlies his precepts. Yet, as we shall see in the next chapter, Confucius gives us only one corner to play with: you and I have to identify the other three corners that make up the square.

KEY POINTS

- Your journey as a leader really progresses when you achieve sufficient clarity about the concept of leadership.

- Leading means showing others the way and taking them with you on the journey by land or sea. It is this same metaphor that gives us the English words *governor* and *government* (from the Greek and Latin words for steersman, who in antiquity was usually both the navigator and ship's captain as well).

- Leadership is an ambiguous term. The suffix *-ship* can mean either position or office (role), or it can denote skill or art (ability). Human society works when those who occupy leadership roles have leadership ability, so it is essential for the world to develop people with leadership ability.

- All languages have a set of names for those who occupy specific roles of leadership, such as (in

English) *head, chief, director, manager, commander.* But underlying all these names there is a universal generic role of *leader,* defined by all people having broadly the same expectations from those in positions of leadership responsibility.

◡ The generic role of *leader* arises from the presence of the three overlapping areas of need – *task, team* and *individual* – in all working groups and the consequent set of practical *functions* required to meet these areas in the contexts of ever-changing environments.

◡ A good leader is someone whom people will follow through thick and thin, in good times and bad, because they have confidence in the leader as a person, the leader's ability and his or her knowledge of the job, and because they know they matter to the leader.

◡ Leadership is done at different levels. The Three Circles model remains constant, but the functions change according to context and tend to become more complex the higher up the ladder of responsibility you go.

Without a leader, the birds do not fly far.

Chinese proverb

2

LEADING FROM IN FRONT

**'You must be the change that you
wish to see in the world.'**
Mahatma Gandhi

Chi K'ang Tzu succeeded his father as the chief minister
in Confucius' native state of Lu in 492 BCE, holding office
for more than twenty-five years. On several occasions he
sought advice from a neighbour already renowned for his
practical wisdom.

> The prevalence of thieves was a source of trouble to
> Chi K'ang Tzu, who asked the advice of Confucius.
> Confucius answered, 'If you yourself were not a man
> of desires, no one would steal even if stealing carried
> a reward.' (12:18)

The phrase 'a man of desires' is rather obscure. In this
context, it probably doesn't mean outright greed, covetous-
ness and corruption. It is more likely that what Confucius

has in mind is the desire to live in great comfort amid lavish surroundings, to be served with fine food and to wear richly embroidered garments. Surely this luxury is the reward for high office?

Confucius seems to be doing some creative social thinking here. He is making a connection between two phenomena which – for most people – are completely separate: on the one hand, the public display of sumptuous living and opulent surroundings indulged in by those of the highest rank, and on the other hand the prevalence of theft among ordinary people. Those who resort to theft or robbery, Confucius argues, are simply following – at one or two removes – the example set by Chi K'ang Tzu and his like.

Perhaps the overwhelming majority of people in law-abiding societies will choose to work hard in lawful ways in order to taste the luxuries of life one day. But there will always be a few 'have nots' who are minded to take the criminal shortcut of stealing from others, whatever the risk to life or limb. If people see those occupying positions of leadership taking their own illegal or immoral shortcuts to wealth – for example, by seeking out bribes or by acting corruptly in other ways – will they not be tempted to follow suit? Of course they will, especially if they see their betters getting away with it. Such is the power of bad example.

Corruption and other forms of financial malpractice – still so prevalent today among leaders of nations – are essentially theft, for a corrupt ruler, minister or official is in effect stealing money from their own people. They are as guilty as a common thief, even though the act takes place in secret and all too often escapes the kind of scrutiny that leads to justice.

Confucius, however, is far more interested in stressing the power of good example. The higher you are, he implies, the longer your shadow – the influence of the example you provide. Given such good example in their leaders, few people will resort to theft or – by extension – to corrupt practices.

And this will be the case even if – Confucius adds, doubtless with a smile – they were offered a considerable reward for doing so. Lao-tzu, the other great authority on leadership in the Chinese tradition, makes the very same point:

> Not to honour men of worth will keep people from contention; not to value goods which are hard to come by will keep them from theft; not to display what is desirable will keep them from being unsettled of mind. (3:8)

Is it true? Does it work? Of course it does. The Prophet Muhammad and the first four caliphs of Islam, for example, led simple lives and were scrupulous in all financial matters, and corruption was unknown in the Muslim states of their day. The first president of Botswana and his three successors set their faces against corruption, and as a result Botswana became the least corrupt nation in Africa.

What both these cases suggest, however, is when it comes to moral leadership in a nation, there is a need for continuity. One Nelson Mandela is never enough.

Confucius sees leadership by example as the natural way of controlling people, far superior to the use of force or compulsion. In this sense, the leader is always a teacher, and example is the sovereign method in the teaching of manners or morals. Confucius would have agreed whole-heartedly with Dr Albert Schweitzer: 'Example is not the main thing in influencing others – it is the only thing.'

Like Confucius, Dr Schweitzer (1875–1965) embodied his own principle: he led by example. Born in the disputed territory of Alsace not long after it was annexed by the German Empire, he decided to devote the first thirty years of his life to learning and music, and the remainder to the service of others. In 1913 he qualified as a medical doctor and went as a missionary to Lambaréné in French Equatorial Africa (now Gabon), where he established a hospital and served there for the rest of his life. In fact, missionary is a misleading term when applied to Schweitzer, for he made no attempt to convert the neighbouring West African tribes or even his grateful patients to any form of Christianity. His call was to serve the cause of the Kingdom of God on earth – a term which meant much the same thing as the Confucian or Taoist 'Way of Heaven' at work in this world. Indeed, the earliest disciples of Jesus were known as followers of 'the Way'. And that Way was the way of love, expressed in practical service to one's neighbour. It was by his example at Lambaréné – by moral leadership – that Schweitzer hoped to advance the reign of mutual love and support among the people. In 1952 he was awarded the Nobel Peace Prize.

As you may have guessed, Schweitzer was something of a boyhood hero to me. As an undergraduate at Cambridge University in 1958, I waited in the freezing rain one winter's day outside the Senate House to catch a glimpse of him as he arrived in procession to receive an honorary degree. I had no camera to record the occasion, but in my mind's eye I can still see his granite-like face and mane of grey hair, and the way he looked inquisitively about him as he walked.

It is one thing to lead by example yourself in this way, and quite another to teach other leaders to follow suit. During another conversation with the chief minister of Lu, Confucius resorted to one of his favourite plays on words:

> Chi K'ang Tzu asked Confucius about government. Confucius answered, 'To govern [*cheng*] is to correct [*cheng*]. If you set an example by being correct, who would dare to remain incorrect?' (12:17)

In those days, rulers had an arbitrary power of life or death over their people, and history is filled with examples of rulers who exercised this prerogative with ruthlessness and cruelty. Chi K'ang Tzu had a more moral purpose in mind. Like modern politicians with only a relatively short period in office to get things done, he was attracted by the lure of short-term solutions, however draconian. Why not use the death penalty, he asked, just to speed up the pace of moral reform? But for Confucius, the end could never justify such means.

> Chi K'ang Tzu asked Confucius about government, saying, 'What would you think if, in order to move closer to those who possess the Way, I were to kill those who do not follow the Way?'
> Confucius answered, 'In administering your government, what need is there for you to kill? Just desire the good yourself and the common people will be good. The virtue of the gentleman is like wind; the virtue of the small man is like grass. Let the wind blow over the grass and it is sure to bend.' (12:19, see also 6:27)

Plainly, Confucius is thinking in terms not of years but of generations. He knows that the influence of sustained moral example works slowly in society, like the agency of yeast in raising bread. A wise leader is patient, like a teacher. Give it time.

Confucius held to be true the saying that after a state

36

has been ruled for a hundred years by good men, it is possible to get the better of cruelty and to do away with killing. Even with a true king, it is bound to take several generations for benevolence – peace and goodwill among men – to take root and become the dominant social reality.

You may have already spotted a flaw in Confucius' theory. Three or four generations of good leaders in government over a century can make a positive difference to society; but what happens if their successor or successors turn out to be bad people?

Confucius believes implicitly that human nature is predominantly good. His greatest successor, Mencius (c. 371–c. 289 BCE), states it much more explicitly: 'Human nature is disposed to do good, just as water flows downwards. There is no man that does not show this tendency to goodness.' But Confucius is fully aware that as individuals we have a nature like a magpie: white and black, good and bad – the two existing side by side or intermingled. Especially in a hereditary system – though democracy carries no immunity – over long stretches of time the likelihood of an individual who is below the norm of goodness coming to power (or seizing it by force) is quite high.

It is not surprising that some of Confucius' more realistic neighbours regarded him as little more than a dreamer or visionary, as this extract shows:

Tzu-lu put up for the night at the Stone Gate. The gatekeeper said, 'Where have you come from?'

37

Tzu-lu said, 'From the Kung family.'

'Is that the Kung who keeps working towards a goal the realization of which he knows to be hopeless?' (14:38)

Personally, I love his optimism. Leaders need always to create a climate of hope; Confucius created hope for China and ultimately for all mankind. And hope is the oxygen of the human spirit. Napoleon spoke truly when he said that a leader is 'a dealer in hope'. Courage is the child of optimism: the courage to keep going and not to give up even when to ordinary eyes life looks quite hopeless.

Confucius was remarkable for being a calm and serene man, at ease with himself and his world. He had faith that in the course of time Heaven would bring about the changes he envisaged; but that was Heaven's work. His task – like yours or mine – is simple: to do his best in the present to bring about the state or conditions on earth which Heaven intended and would bring about in its own good time. In the meantime, there is no need to be anxious about the future – just do your best.

Confucius, in fact, had plenty of first-hand experience of bad or incompetent leaders. Furthermore, he knew that if nothing changed, China, like the rest of the world, could expect an unending procession of mediocre people occupying positions of authority, relieved only by the occasional outstandingly good leader or really bad tyrant. The solution, he believed, lay in education – in educating the rising generation for *good leadership and leadership for good*.

In the history of the world, particularly in the history of scientific discovery, great ideas sometimes seem to arise at more or less the same time but quite independently. A famous scientific example is the theory of evolution, which seems to have developed in the minds of Charles Darwin and Arthur Wallace concurrently. Confucius' great idea – training for leadership – had such a counterpart in distant Greece. While Confucius was just a boy, Cleisthenes had given Athens its first democratic constitution. It didn't take too long for young Athenians to discover that they now needed to know how they could persuade their fellow citizens to elect them as leaders. As it happened, they were fortunate to find a great teacher of leadership, the man they called 'the Thinker' – Socrates.

Socrates was born in 469 BCE, just ten years after the death of Confucius. Like Confucius, he was adept at getting his students to think for themselves. He gave no formal lectures; it was by conversation with him that his students learnt about life and leadership. Indeed, his two greatest disciples, Plato and Xenophon, reflected this method by writing their books in the form of what the Greeks called dialogue, setting out conversations between Socrates and two or more persons.

If we look at the works of Plato and Xenophon, it is fairly clear what Socrates had to say about leadership. In a society of free and equal persons, he argues, leadership should be given to those who have the ability to lead. That fitness to lead certainly included a moral element – it would have been self-evidently perverse for the Athenians, or any other society for that matter, to elect a morally bad man to be a leader. But Socrates and his disciples are distinguished by the emphasis that they put upon knowledge as the key. It seemed to them an empirical fact that in any field it was natural for men to defer to those superior to them in professional or technical knowledge and experience. The first requirement for a leader, then, is to know your business. *Authority flows to the one who knows.*

Yet there is more to being a leader than simply knowing more than everyone else in the room. Xenophon (*c.* 435–*c.* 354 BCE) is the true founder of what we would call today the scientific study of leadership – the tradition that eventually produced the Three Circles model and the generic role of leader concepts outlined in Chapter 1. For Xenophon was the first person to observe leaders in action and to try to identify the principles that governed their success or failure – the scientific or empirical method.

Xenophon could also draw upon considerable personal experience, both as a general – he was elected to that office at the age of twenty-six in the middle of a disastrous campaign in Persia – and later as a businessman running an estate. He was the first thinker to realize that there were transferable functions of leadership, even arguing that because of them it would be possible for a successful businessman to become a *strategos* (a general, literally in Greek 'the leader of an army'). Here is his composite

40

portrait of the inspiring leader in any field of human enterprise:

> For some commanders make their men unwilling to work and take risks, disinclined and unwilling to obey, except under compulsion, and actually proud of defying their commander. Yes, and these commanders cause these men to have no sense of dishonour when something disgraceful happens.
>
> Contrast the brave and skilful general with a natural gift for leadership. Let him take over command of these same troops or of others if you like. What effect has he on them? They are ashamed to do a disgraceful act, think it better to obey and take pride in obedience, working cheerfully – each man and all together – when it is necessary to work.
>
> Just as a love of work may spring up in the mind of a private soldier here and there, so a whole army under the influence of a good leader is inspired by love of work and ambition to distinguish itself under the commander's eye. If this is the feeling of the rank and file for their commander, then he is an excellent leader.
>
> So leadership is not a matter of being best with bow and javelin, nor riding the best horse and being foremost in danger, nor being the most knowledgeable about cavalry tactics. It is being able to make his soldiers feel that they must follow him through fire and in any adventure.

The same is true of private industries: the man in authority – the director or manager – who can make the workers eager, industrious and persevering – he is the man who grows the business in a profitable way.

On a warship, when out on the high seas and the rowers must toil all day to reach port, some rowing masters can say and do the right thing to raise the men's spirits and make them work with a will. Other rowing masters are so lacking in this ability that it takes them twice the time to finish the same voyage. Here they land bathed in sweat, with mutual congratulations, master and oarsmen. There they arrive with dry skin; they hate their master and he hates them.

The strength of Xenophon is that he only teaches what he knows by experience works in practice. Leadership is a practical subject. Hence the Ugandan proverb: *The best person to teach leadership is a leader.* Xenophon knows what he is talking about when he writes: 'There is a small risk that leaders will be regarded with contempt by those they lead if whatever they ask of others they show themselves best able to perform.' It is no wonder that Xenophon's books on the nature and practice of leadership were avidly read in the Greek and Roman worlds. Alexander the Great, Hannibal, Scipio Africanus (the victor over Hannibal), Julius Caesar and Cicero were among those who studied what he had to say on the subject – quite a readership! The principle set out by him above – leading from the front, being capable or willing to do yourself what you ask others to do – is as valid today as it was for Xenophon and his readers. Why? Because human nature remains much the same; the differences wrought by our time in history or our location on earth are relatively minor. Confucius says as much:

> The Master said, 'Men are close to one another by nature. They diverge as a result of repeated practice.' (17:2)

In physics, the speed of light is a constant. By analogy, our 'closeness' of human nature is also a social constant, and it determines why the laws of good leadership work universally. For this same reason, as Confucius famously taught, we can safely use ourselves as a gauge for knowing how to behave to others. For if we know ourselves, we know what works for others too. A simple principle, to be sure, but one that has stood the test of time.

In the field of leadership, this principle can be applied by not leading others in a way that you would resent being led yourself. With a little bit of practice, you will find that you already know intuitively how someone in a position of leadership should lead other people. (Perhaps I shouldn't have told you that, as you may stop buying my books!) That is why a period of being in a role serving under a leader is always valuable experience for a person who will one day be a leader himself or herself. One of Xenophon's readers, the Roman statesman and writer

Cicero (106–43 BCE), puts it this way: 'The man who commands efficiently must have obeyed others in the past, and the man who obeys dutifully is worthy of some day being a commander.'

But it is not merely the skill of giving effective orders that a potential leader will learn as a subordinate. He also discovers the kind of leadership that draws the very best out of him – as well as, conversely, the non-leadership that drains his vital energies and causes the flame of his spirit to flicker and fade. Following Confucius, he will then have learnt what others expect of him when he finally takes upon himself the role of *leader* and they turn to look towards him.

The Socratic principle that it is knowledge that best fits a person for leadership in any field of human enterprise paved the way for the rise of the great schools and universities of the West. When Britain, for example, acquired a great empire, it was the British public schools and universities, inspired by the Greek and Roman writings on leadership, that supplied its governors, administrators, military commanders and teachers.

Inspired largely by Confucius, China adopted a system of fair and open appointments to administrative office hundreds of years before this became common practice in the West. Competitive examinations for civil servants were introduced as early as the Han dynasty of emperors

(206 BCE–220 CE). To become a a Chinese official, or Mandarin, it was necessary to pass a gruelling set of examinations, sometimes lasting as long as seventy-two hours, in such subjects as arithmetic, knowledge of ritual and ceremonies, military strategies, civil law and, of course, the Confucian classics. Pass rates were so poor (as low as 2 per cent during the Tang dynasty of 618–907 CE) that some candidates would sit exams annually into their old age. Others committed suicide, unable to bear the disgrace of continual failure.

'It is certain,' Shakespeare wrote in *Henry IV, Part Two*, 'that either wise bearing or ignorant carriage is caught, as men take diseases, therefore let men take heed of their company.' In the West no less than in the East, or in tribal societies, the power of moral – or immoral – example has always been well understood. In Christendom the failure of spiritual leaders to lead from in front – by good example – always troubled the best minds. As Shakespeare puts it:

> Do not like some ungracious pastors do,
> Show us the steep and thorny way to heaven,
> While they the primrose path of dalliance tread
> And reck [follow] not their own rede [advice].

Pope Gregory the Great (*c.* 540–604 CE) did his best to recall these 'ungracious pastors' to their calling as leaders. He wrote a handbook of rules for pastors – meaning 'of shepherds' in Latin – in which he declared:

> The ruler should be exemplary in his conduct, that by his manner of life he may show the way of life to his subjects, and that the flock, following the teaching and conduct of its shepherd, may proceed the better through example rather than words.
>
> For one who by the necessity of his position must propose the highest ideals, is bound by that same necessity to give demonstration of those ideals. His voice penetrates the hearts of his hearers the more readily, if his way of life commends what he says.

Confucius himself could not have expressed it more clearly. These words apply to all leaders, especially those who by calling are both in the public service and in the public eye.

KEY POINTS

- Leadership is done from in front. You shouldn't show others the way unless you are willing to go there yourself. A leader says 'Come on', not 'Go on'. Without example, leadership lacks moral authority.

- A corrupt politician, official or businessman is as much a thief as a small-time burglar. They are stealing from the people they are there to serve. Political crime breeds petty crime.

- ☽ Example – good or bad – is contagious. Many proverbs attest to this fact, for example: *A frightened captain makes a frightened crew.* Or, as they say in Africa: *If the leader limps, all the others start limping too.*

- ☽ Word and example should always go hand in hand. 'He that gives good advice builds with one hand,' wrote Francis Bacon. 'He that gives good counsel and example builds with both. But he that gives good admonition and bad example, builds with one hand and pulls down with the other.'

- ☽ The influence of good example takes time to work – maybe years. So you need patience to be a leader, together with a long-term perspective on your work. And great leaders need great optimism.

- ☽ Leading from in front wins more than respect – it eventually attracts love. And love is true power. As Huainanzi wrote in a classic Taoist text:

In ancient times good generals always were in the vanguard themselves. They didn't set up canopies in the heat and didn't wear leather in the cold; thus they experienced the same heat and cold as their soldiers.

They did not ride over rough terrain, always dismounting when climbing hills; thus they experienced the same toil as their soldiers.

They would eat only after food had been cooked for the troops, and they would drink only after water had been drawn for the troops; thus they experienced the same hunger and thirst as their soldiers.

In battle they would stand within range of enemy fire; thus they experienced the same dangers as their soldiers.

So in their military operations, good generals always use accumulated gratitude to attack accumulated bitterness, and accumulated love to attack accumulated hatred. Why would they not win?

Those who are near will not hide their ability, and those who are distant will not grumble at their toil ... That is what is called being a leader and teacher of men.

3

ACHIEVING THE TASK

'An army of a thousand is easy to find,
but how difficult to find a general.'
Chinese proverb

The thousand soldiers in the above proverb are expected to fight with courage and skill. They are honoured for doing so whatever the outcome of the war: they will have done their duty and thus achieved their personal task. Not so the general. He is judged by whether or not he delivers victory. For the general is clearly in the role of *leader*. He is accountable for success in the 'Task' needs circle. Therefore his chief priority is *achieving the task*. In the case of a commander-in-chief, that means victory. If he fails to deliver victory, he will be replaced sooner or later by another more promising general.

The basic Three Circles model, as you can see, does in fact give us *three* broad overlapping areas of functional activity, not just one. But the 'Task' circle is the first in importance, and when the model is drawn correctly it should always appear as the top circle.

Areas of functional responsibility.

To achieve the task, build and maintain the team, and motivate and develop the individual, however, certain key *functions* need to be effectively performed – such as *defining the task, planning, controlling* and *coordinating, supporting, providing an example* and *evaluating*. These necessary leadership functions are normally set out as a single list, because their performance – or malperformance – always affects more than one circle. Failure on the part of a leader to define the common task, for example, tends to divide the team and to cause individuals frustration.

Again, the model emphasizes that it is ultimately what you *do* effectively as a leader that counts, not what you *know* or *are*.

Confucius didn't have our advantage of having the leadership model before him, but he certainly wanted leaders to be action-centred.

> The Master said, 'There is nothing I can do with a man who is not constantly saying 'What am I to do? What am I to do?' (15:16)

He often contrasts those who are content to talk in a clever or facile way with what the English call a 'doer' – a person who *does* something, a person who acts rather than merely talks. The preference of Confucius is plain:

> Tzu-kung asked about the gentleman. The Master said, 'He puts his words into action before allowing his words to follow his action.' (2:13)

A leader should be ashamed of his word outstripping his deed (14:27). Confucius once claimed that he had learnt to judge people by their actions, not their words, as a result of his experiences with Tsai Yü, not one of the brighter stars in the Kung household school.

Tsai Yü was in bed in the daytime. The Master said, 'A piece of rotten wood cannot be carved, nor can a wall of dried dung be trowelled. As far as Yü is concerned what is the use of condemning him?'

The Master added, 'I used to take on trust a man's deeds after having listened to his words. Now having listened to a man's words I go on to observe his deeds. It was on account of Yü that I have changed in this respect.' (5:10)

The Duke of Wellington, famous for defeating Napoleon at the Battle of Waterloo, once attributed his success in life to 'doing the day's business in the day'. In other words, he never procrastinated by putting off action and making empty excuses for doing so. Confucius always admired the spirit of *no sooner said than done*. Of his disciple Tzu-lu – quite the opposite of the wretched Tsai Yü – he once said with admiration: 'Tzu-lu never put off the fulfilment of a promise to the next day' (12:12).

The function I have called *defining the task* calls for some explanation. *Task* is a general word in this context; it means something that needs to be done. No one can achieve *task* in the abstract; it is always a specific task. It may be self-evident as to what it is, like reaching the summit of Mount Everest for a team of climbers. Or the task may be – to follow the metaphor – shrouded in mist, so ambiguous or vague that the team cannot even begin to work towards it. In situations such as this, the leader needs to ensure that the function of *defining the task* is performed effectively.

Confucius himself performs this particular leadership function in relation to the work of government. The purpose of government, he says, is the good of the people. That sounds simple and perhaps commonplace to us, but as far as I can tell, no one in human history had actually said this before.

Serving the welfare of the common people begins with ensuring that their basic needs are satisfied: 'Tzu-kung asked about government. The Master said, "Give them enough food"' (12:7). In order to achieve this first step, the common people must be free to labour in the fields at key times; they must not be taken away from working the land except in the right seasons (1:5). One Tzu-ch'an was held up as a model for aspiring leaders: he was 'generous in caring for the people and just in employing their services' (5:16).

Confucius offers us no definition of the good of the people, and perhaps there is no need for one. If pressed, however, he would have doubtless agreed with this simple definition given by the famous Scottish poet Robert Burns: 'Whatever mitigates the woes or increases the happiness of others, this is my criterion of goodness; and whatever injures society at large, or any individual in it, this is my measure of iniquity.'

According to Confucius, resources are there to be used for the good of others – even resources that come unexpectedly to hand by way of a gift:

On becoming his [Confucius'] steward, Yüan Ssu was given nine hundred measures of grain which he declined. The Master said, 'Can you not find a use for it in helping the people in your neighbourhood?' (6:5)

In team or corporate affairs it is necessary for a leader to be able to break down the common *purpose* into more specific *aims*, and then those aims into attainable *objectives*, and finally these *objectives* into *steps* that can be taken daily. As the proverb says: *An elephant can be eaten only one mouthful at a time.*

Coming down the ladder from the general to the particular answers the question *How*: how are we going to achieve our common *purpose*? Answer: by achieving these *aims*. And how are we going to achieve this particular *aim*? Answer: by attaining these *objectives*.

If you reverse direction and, so to speak, go up the ladder, you are in effect answering the question *Why*: why are we looking towards this *objective*? Answer: in order to achieve this *aim*. And why this *aim*? In order to achieve our common *purpose*.

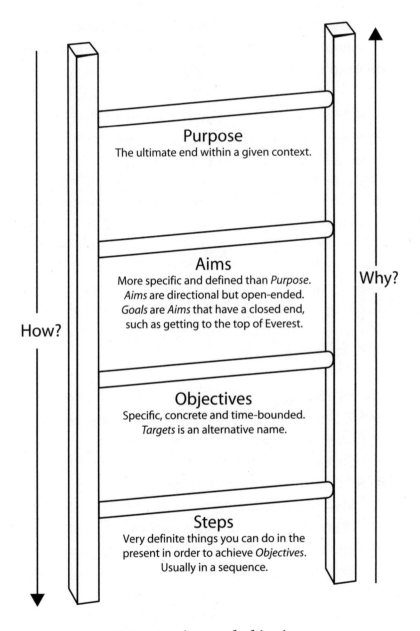

How?

Why?

Purpose
The ultimate end within a given context.

Aims
More specific and defined than *Purpose*.
Aims are directional but open-ended.
Goals are *Aims* that have a closed end,
such as getting to the top of Everest.

Objectives
Specific, concrete and time-bounded.
Targets is an alternative name.

Steps
Very definite things you can do in the
present in order to achieve *Objectives*.
Usually in a sequence.

Purpose, aims and objectives.

Having a sense of a wider or greater purpose prevents you from ever running out of ideas about what to do next. An objective achieved or goal attained is never the end of the story for a true leader. 'It is provided in the essence of things,' said Walt Whitman, 'that from any fraction of success, no matter what, shall come further something to make a great struggle necessary.'

Success in achieving short-term targets all too often breeds failure where leaders lack foresight and vision. An organization without leaders with these qualities can be in danger of sitting back and resting on its laurels. True leaders, however, always have one eye on the next horizon. By coming up with new goals, they keep people continually looking and moving forwards on their journey to what Shakespeare calls 'undiscovered ends'. Confucius exemplifies this imaginative power.

> When the Master went to Wei, Jan Yu drove for him. The Master said, 'What a flourishing population!'
>
> Jan Yu said, 'When the population is flourishing, what further benefit can one add?'
>
> 'Make the people rich.'
>
> 'When the people have become rich, what further benefit can one add?'
>
> 'Train them.' (13:9)

As Marie Curie (1867–1934), pioneer of radioactivity, who received two Nobel Prizes for physics and chemistry, once said to a friend: 'One never notices what has been done; one can only see what remains to be done.' And a leader almost by definition does know what to do. As Winston Churchill once said, 'An accepted leader has only to be sure of what it is best to do, or at least to have made up his mind about it.'

Incidentally, by 'training the people' Confucius had rather more in mind than equipping them with the relatively simple military drills and skills required by foot soldiers of the day. He says elsewhere that it will take seven years – in other words, it is a long-term project. He gives us no programme, but it must have included the rudiments of physical, mental and moral education. Modern China's passion for education and technical training of all sorts is a distant reflection of what was once the gleam in Confucius' visionary eye.

The function of *defining the task* is not the only function that Confucius teaches. Clearly he attached great importance to *planning* where any common enterprise is concerned.

Planning is indeed a major leadership function. That doesn't mean to say that the leader should do all the planning himself; merely that he is responsible for seeing that a feasible plan has been made. For, as the old saying goes, 'failing to plan is planning to fail'.

Planning entails step-by-step or sequential thinking. It

is a transferable mental skill. Shakespeare gives us an example of this transferability in his play *Henry IV, Part Two*, when the conspirator Lord Bardolph compares planning an armed rebellion to building a house. In both instances, Bardolph points out, no reliance must be placed on 'conjectures, expectation and surmise', still less on a vague hope that things will somehow work out all right.

> When we mean to build,
> We first survey the plot, then draw the model.
> And when we see the figure of the house,
> Then must we rate the cost of the erection,
> Which if we find outweighs ability,
> What do we do then but draw anew the model
> In fewer offices, or at least desist
> To build at all?

Confucius obviously gave much thought to the need for planning. Doubtless some past experience of rulers or ministers getting things wrong lay behind his comment: 'To attack a task from the wrong end can do nothing but harm'. To tackle any task out of sequence in this way is, of course, symptomatic of poor planning.

All the best leaders are, in Confucius' words, 'fond of making plans'.

> Tzu-lu said, 'If you were leading the Three Armies whom would you take with you?'
> The Master said, 'I would not take with me any-

one who would try to fight a tiger with his bare hands or to walk across the River and die in the process without regrets. If I took anyone it would have to be a man who, when faced with a task, was fearful of failure and who, while fond of making plans, was capable of successful execution.' (7:11)

Confucius is not an 'either/or' thinker, but a 'both/and' one. He wants a leader who *both* applies himself to careful planning *and* is also skilled in making it happen. Execution – making it happen – is so often the least well-performed function in strategic leadership.

Flexibility is essential in both planning and execution. As a general once said to me, 'A plan is a very good basis for changing your mind.' Confucius had a passion for flexibility. True, he did have some admiration for the man 'who insists on keeping his word and seeing his actions through to the end ... even though he shows a stubborn petty-mindedness' (13:20). But a good leader should aspire to be both determined and tenacious when it comes to achieving ends, while remaining infinitely flexible over means.

Plans should be firmly made, but not set in concrete. A change of plan should arise naturally, usually because new facts have come to light, and not as a result of a sudden attack of nerves resulting in indecision. Changing plans for no reason always carries the risk of breeding an atmosphere of uncertainty. And a plan should never be changed beyond the 'point of no return' – that is, the point in time when the disorder and confusion caused by changing the plan will outweigh any possible benefits to be gained by improving it. Remember the sequence: *order, counter-order, disorder.*

Nor should planning be allowed to go on too long, leading to the postponement of necessary action. There is always a danger in leadership of spending too much time with your team or colleagues in planning, forgetting that there is no such thing as a perfect plan. Winston Churchill once counselled: 'Do not let the better be the enemy of the good.' And he added: 'The maxim "Nothing avails but perfection": can be spelt shorter, "Paralysis".' Yet you do not want to rush ahead without taking sufficient thought. Confucius counsels us to use our judgement over planning, to aim for the golden mean.

> Chi Wen Tzu always thought three times before taking action. When the Master was told of this, he commented, 'Twice is quite enough.' (5:20)

In both phases of planning and execution, Confucius always advocates the advantages of breaking down bigger tasks into small ones – the step-by-step approach. However, he adds, you should avoid the danger of becoming so absorbed in short-term gains that you take your eye off the larger and more challenging tasks that belong to your role and responsibilities as a leader. The military principle of *selecting and*

maintaining the aim is a useful one for all leaders to bear in mind. In the tribal tradition of leadership, the same idea is expressed in more homely proverbial language: *Deer-hunter, do not waste your arrows on the birds.*

When it comes to dismantling tasks into achievable steps, the Master practised what he preached. One thing that impressed his disciples was his skill in breaking down the uphill path of learning into steps. They felt that he was leading them forward on the journey step by step:

> Yen Yüan, heaving a sigh, said, 'The more I look up at it the higher it appears. The more I bore into it the harder it becomes. I see it before me. Suddenly it is behind me.
>
> 'The Master is good at leading one on step by step. He broadens me with culture and brings me back to essentials by means of the rites. I cannot give up even if I wanted to, but, having done all I can, it seems to rise sheer above me and I have no way of going after it, however, much I may want to.' (9:11)

In fact, Confucius never sets the bar too high, though some of his less able students did feel at times that he was asking the impossible of them. He believed education should be tailored to an individual's innate level of aptitude.

> The Master said, 'You can tell those who are above average about the best, but not those who are below average.' (6:21)

But Confucius did not care for students who gave up on the journey because they found the uphill struggle for self-improvement too hard for them. We owe to Lao-tzu the celebrated Chinese proverb: *The journey of a thousand miles begins with a single step.* Confucius, however, characteristically insists upon the importance of the *last* step, the follow-through that crowns successful execution. Every step in the right direction takes us forward, but the task is not completed until the final step has been taken:

> The Master said, 'As in the case of making a mound, if, before the very last basketful, I stop, then I shall have stopped. As in the case of levelling the ground, if, though tipping only one basketful, I am going forward, then I shall be making progress.' (9:19)

Confucius' insistence on the importance of taking that last step – finishing the job – is worth underlining, for so often in human affairs there is a lack of follow-through, a failure to complete what you have set out to do. Sir Francis Drake (*c.* 1540–96) was the first English sailor to circumnavigate the globe. In 1577 he set sail with five ships to investigate the Strait of Magellan, then he tried unsuccessfully to find the North-West Passage, and finally ended his great voyage with a triumphant return to England in 1580 by way of the Cape of Good Hope. There was just one ship left out of his original squadron. He wrote in a letter from the *Golden Hind*: 'There must be a beginning of any great matter, but the continuing unto the end until it be thoroughly finished yields the true glory.'

It is easy to have conferences and meetings, to engage in strategic thinking and planning, but all too often the execution phase seems to present unforeseeable and apparently insurmountable difficulties to all but the most determined of leaders. Karl von Clausewitz (1780–1831), Prussian general and military theorist, is the most famous writer on generalship in the West. He lacks the insight and poetry of his great Chinese counterpart Sun Tzu, but he spoke from experience when he wrote in *On War* (1833): 'Everything in war is very simple, but the simplest thing is difficult. The difficulties accumulate and end by producing a kind of friction that is inconceivable unless one has experienced war.'

Sometimes one can sense Confucius' frustration at not being given the highest office available to a commoner in his day. Being a chief minister in a state would have given him a real opportunity to demonstrate that his approach to governmental leadership would work in practice. Certainly Confucius had one quality essential for the holder of such an office, one that is a foundation for leadership: self-confidence.

> The Master said, 'If anyone were to employ me, in a year's time I would have brought things to a satisfactory state, and after three years I should have results to show for it.' (13:10)

Fortunately for us, Heaven had a different destiny in mind for Confucius. How many chief ministers of his time are remembered today? But the action-centred spirit of Confucius – his desire to *do* the work of leadership, rather than merely teach it to others – reminds us that he could teach leadership to others because in his innermost spirit he was a leader himself.

KEY POINTS

- Central to the role of *leader* is the expectation that he will enable others to *achieve the task*. Leaders who fail to deliver success in this area of responsibility will seldom survive for long.

- All the functions performed by an action-centred leader relate either directly or indirectly to achieving the task, both at the stages of *planning* and *execution*.

- Achieving the task calls for decision-making. Give careful thought when making decisions, but don't waste time by thinking too much. Remember the Chinese proverb: *He who thinks too much about everything will stay on one leg all his life.*

- Always remain flexible and be willing to adjust your plan as you implement it. 'One thing is sure,' said President F.D. Roosevelt. 'We have to do something. We have to do the best we know how at the moment. If it doesn't turn out right, we can modify it as we go along.'

☾ Never fear that you will run out of tasks to achieve. The art of leadership is always to see the next summit to be climbed on the horizon, always to prepare people for the greater challenges that lie ahead.

You have not done enough, you have never done enough, so long as it is still possible that you have something of value to contribute.

Dag Hammarskjöld, addressing himself as
Secretary-General of the United Nations
in his journal, Markings

4

BUILDING THE TEAM

**'When people are of one mind and heart,
they can move Mount Tai.'***
Chinese proverb

What does a leader do? Apart from working to achieve the
task, he builds a team, helps to hold it together and develops
harmonious teamwork. As the picture of the Three Circles
model tells us, the two functional areas of the task and the
team are interactive – for good or ill. Failure to achieve the
common task, for example, has a disintegrating effect upon
relations in the group: the centrifugal forces in the group
dynamics are accentuated and the team will tend to fall
apart. Conversely, a group of quarrelling and mutually
suspicious individuals, entirely lacking in team spirit, are
unlikely to achieve any demanding or worthwhile task.

More than once Confucius shows an awareness of the

***

* Tai is a mountain in what is now the Shandong Province, the largest
one known to Confucius.

importance of teamwork in government. What he usually has in mind is the group of ministers who, under the guidance of the chief minister, performed the functions of government we are familiar with today, such as public administration, the maintenance of law and order, and the conduct of diplomacy. But the 'one corner of a square' Confucius gives us can be developed into an insight about the generic role of *leader* in relation to the second circle of responsibility: *building the team*.

What is a team? The origin of the Old English word *team* provides us with a clue: a set of draught animals, such as oxen, horses or dogs, harnessed together to pull a vehicle or implement. The word literally meant offspring or lineage, probably because it was found that animals pulled together better if they were related. So teamwork here is the combined action of a group of individuals, its drawing or pulling power. Notice that the importance of selection is already in the picture: only a *well-matched* group of animals produces teamwork that is effective and efficient.

At the level of human society, a team is a number of persons who associate together in work or activity to achieve a purpose. Again, the emphasis is upon the combined effort that produces the desired result, which is far beyond what any of the individual members working alone can achieve. Many proverbs testify to the value of combining our talents and efforts; I particularly like the Ethiopian version: *When spiders unite they can tie up a lion.* Among the Chinese equivalents we find: *If people are of one heart, even the yellow earth can become gold.*

Each of us has a body, and our body serves as a kind of personal reminder about the complementary nature of advanced teamwork. For our bodies are composed of various *members*, such as eyes and ears, hands and feet, each of which has its own distinctive functions, yet they are clearly complementary. We are wholes rather than collections of spare parts. Our different members work together in a natural unity and harmony, enabling us to live, move, work and have our being.

The higher level of teamwork in our practical social life reflects this principle of being different-but-complementary and working together as a whole. Here is a simple example from a Chinese fable:

> A certain country was invaded by its enemy. When a lame man there told a blind man of this, the blind man carried the lame one on his back and they escaped together. They did this by making use of each other's strong points.
>
> *Huainanzi*

The same principle can often be found at work in the institution of marriage. Although a couple may be very alike – say in terms of their social background, common interests or shared values – the roles of husband and wife, father and mother prove to be over time both different and complementary. And in a happy marriage the sum of the whole is always greater than the parts.

Thus in any human team, at the higher level – that is, above the basic physical level of a 'tug of war' in which two teams of contestants lay hold of a strong rope and pull against each other until one side has tugged the other over the dividing line – there will be differences in the relative strengths, such as knowledge, know-how or skills, that each member contributes to the whole. But these strengths don't exist or interact in a disembodied way, like chemical elements. They are embodied in persons. And persons – unless they are degraded to the level of draught animals by being made into galley slaves or the like – are free and equal in spirit by birthright. They are free to cooperate or to refuse to do so. They are free to give their best or to withhold their efforts and withdraw into themselves. And, being persons ourselves, we know this to be the case. That is why a team that wants to achieve a task will naturally look for a good leader, one who will stir up within us our natural desire to cooperate together in order to achieve worthwhile ends.

One expression of the principle of complementarity is that we tend to see the fundamental roles in life as coming in pairs: for example, husband and wife, father and son, king and subject, doctor and patient, teacher and pupil, officer and soldier.

Notice that in all these relationships there is always a third element, which is often assumed, disguised or hidden. For all these relations are about something – and that is what I mean by the third factor. The two parties are in effect, consciously or unconsciously, working together towards some purpose or end. They are, so to speak, not looking at each other but outwards, towards that common end. Probably all personal relations are ternary in this sense rather than binary. The French writer and aviator Antoine de Saint-Exupéry (1900–44) gives this principle poetic expression in his book *Wind, Sand and Stars*:

> Once we are bound to our brothers by a common good that is outside us, then we can breathe. Experience teaches us that love is not to gaze at one another but to gaze in the same direction. There is no comradeship except through unity on the same rope, climbing towards the same peak.

Complementary teams of two or more people only achieve their optimum level of effectiveness and efficiency if everyone pulls their weight. That phrase comes from rowing: an oarsman who doesn't put all his weight into the stroke is a drag on the rest of the crew, being in some degree a passenger. Success depends upon each member of the team playing their full part, doing the very best they can.

According to the military proverb, *There are no bad soldiers, only bad officers.* This is a good stimulus for officers to get their act together as leaders, but it is really only a half-truth. For there *are* bad soldiers. Equally, you can find in the pages of military history plenty of examples of good soldiers under bad officers – lions led by donkeys. The winning combination, of course, is a matter of common sense: *good soldiers led by good officers.* As Euripides wrote long ago, 'Ten good soldiers wisely led will beat a hundred without a head.'

Remember that if you succeed as a leader it will be largely because of your team. As the Chinese say: *Behind every able man there are always other able men.*

Is there a complementary role to the generic role of *leader*, as in father and son, doctor and patient? An obvious candidate in English is the word *follower*, which derives from the original metaphor of a party on a journey: a leader going in front and showing the way with the others following in his footsteps – the followers. And in recent years a school of American writers has arisen who have attempted to create a balancing role for which they coined the new word *followership*.*

There are, however, problems in going down this road. To say merely that someone is a follower of another doesn't tell us very much. He may be following the other person intending to kill him! Moreover, followership has a passive ring to it, conjuring up a picture of sheep meekly following behind a shepherd. More seriously, *follower* can suggest someone whose prime loyalty is to the person of a leader –

---

* For more about this school, see Barbara Kellerman, *Followership: How Followers Are Creating Change and Changing Leaders* (Harvard Business School Press, 2008).

perhaps a blind loyalty. Unfortunately Hitler attracted many such followers in his day. Although personal loyalty – follower to leader and leader to follower – has its place, it should never overshadow the primary loyalty of all to the common purpose. Perhaps fellowship would be a better term than followership. For *fellow*, the English word for a man or boy, originally meant a 'fee-layer', that is one who lays down money in a joint venture. In a team, all are fellows in the sense of being sharers or joint investors of time and talent in some form of common enterprise. Shakespeare puts that idea into poetry in the inspiring address his ideal leader of men King Henry V delivers just before the battle of Agincourt:

> We few, we happy few, we band of brothers;
> For he today that sheds his blood with me
> Shall be my brother.

Incidentally, we know what King Henry actually said on that day. He commanded the men carrying the banners to advance, and then shouted out to the soldiers: 'Come on, fellows!' Confucius would have admired his brevity.

Nor can *team member* serve as a name for a person who is in the complementary role to *leader*. The problem here is that the leader is also a team member, and so it doesn't do the work of definition. All are team members or associates, each doing their part. The part of the leader is specific; the roles of the other team members less so. A common requirement is that they set aside any seeking of personal prominence in favour of the effectiveness of the whole.

When we think of teams, we tend to picture the whole team working together, like a football team playing in a match. But there are *sequential* teams as well, whose skills are applied in a sequence. In this case, the team may not be physically working together in the same place.

When you stay in a hotel or hospital, for example, you meet the members of the team in sequence: you never see them all together. Remember, however, that you tend to judge such a hotel or hospital team by its weakest link – that is, the one team member who treats you with discourtesy or incompetence.

Confucius knew the value of *sequential* teamwork. He gives us one vivid example of it drawn from his experience as a minister entrusted more than once with diplomatic missions:

> In composing the text of a treaty, P'i Ch'en would write the draft, Shih Shu would make comments, Tzu-Yü, the master of protocol, would touch it up and Tzu-ch'an of Tung Li would make embellishments. (14:8)

China became famous at an early date for its production of its unique translucent ceramics, known as porcelain.

Some seventy sequential skills were employed in the manufacture and distribution of the sets of fine porcelain tableware produced in China. Similar sets of sequential skills were used in the casting of bronze bells and other objects – a flourishing industry in Confucian times. It was the mastery of complementary teamworking skills deployed in sequence to produce an end product that gave China such an edge in early technology.

From his experience of politics and government, Confucius remarks upon the difference between *associations* and *cliques*. An association for Confucius is a group of people organized for a joint purpose (so a team, as we have seen above, is a form of association). By contrast, a small group of people who come together without a noble end is a clique. The name in English suggests narrow self-interest coupled with an arrogant exclusiveness. Associations are essential, for without teamwork we achieve nothing, but negative cliques are to be avoided:

> The Master said, 'The gentleman enters into associations but not cliques; the small man enters into cliques but not associations.' (2:14)

For Confucius, as for us, a true association entails a community of values. Those who are pursuing radically different ends, he argues, have no need to associate together, or to exchange advice – what have they to talk to each other about?

> The Master said, 'There is no point in people taking counsel together who follow different ways.' (15.40)

And when thinking of association Confucius is never far from his old song, namely that goodness or natural virtue is the foundation of all enduring personal and professional relations. This principle is to be followed in friendship, he teaches: 'Do not accept as friend anyone who is not as good as you' (9:25).

All working groups are subject to group dynamics: forces that are pushing them apart and counter forces that are holding them together. If the group is to retain a cohesive unity – the basis for being an effective working team – the centripetal forces that are pulling them together need to be stronger over time than the centrifugal ones that are driving them apart.

Leaders have a critical role to play in this drama. They should not be divisive figures, agents of the disruptive forces, but rather symbols and agents of unity. For example, they shouldn't appear to favour one sub-group over another, or do or say things that might feed dissent, discord or disunity.

A wise leader will stay close to his group and keep his

antennae out. He develops a sixth sense of what is going on in the team – the state of play as far as its group dynamics are concerned. If he senses that a problem is developing, one that if left unchecked might lead to serious division between group members, he is then in a good position to intervene and nip in the bud the trouble that is taking root. Confucius clearly endorses taking this kind of preventative action before things come to a head:

> The Master said, 'In hearing litigation, I am no different from any other man. But if you insist on a difference, it is, perhaps, that I try to get the parties not to resort to litigation in the first place.' (12:13)

How often a good leader can head off trouble by taking aside one or two team members and having some quiet words with them.

The true test of a team – its moral fibre as well as its professional ability – comes in time of crisis. One particular form of crisis comes when there is a sudden leadership vacuum, either because of a temporary interregnum or because the person occupying the position or office of leader goes completely off the rails, demonstrating beyond all doubt his incompetence or unfitness for office. Only a great team can cope with such a crisis:

When the Master spoke of the total lack of moral principle on the part of Duke Ling of Wei, K'ang Tzu commented, 'That being the case, how is it he did not lose his state?'

Confucius said, 'Chung'shu Yü was responsible for foreign visitors, Priest T'uo for the ancestral temple and Wang-sun Chia for military affairs. That being the case, what question could there have been of his losing his state?' (14:19)

It is said that a child goes through four stages of development in relation to his parents: *dependence, counter-dependence, independence* and *interdependence*. If a team is *dependent* on a leader in a childish way, it falls to pieces when he withdraws. The best of all teams, however, are *interdependent*. They function best with a good leader, but they can function well for a time without one.

KEY POINTS

- ☾ You cannot launch a ship on your own. It calls for teamwork: combining individual strengths and pulling power in a common effort.

- ☾ Greater synergy and effectiveness are achieved when complementary abilities, skills or strengths are blended together. These skills may be applied together or in sequence – often teams are not physically working together at the same time.

- *Even a goat and ox must keep in step if they are to plough together.* For any form of effective teamwork, an acceptance of a common aim, some agreement on operational rules and harmony of spirit are all essential. That is why teams need leaders.

- An *esprit de corps* grows in the best teams: a feeling of devotion to the group and pride in belonging to it.

- *One arrow on its own can be easily broken, but not a bundle of ten.* This Japanese proverb reminds us that belonging to a team is a source of mutual strength and support. It meets our individual social needs, as well as enabling us to achieve great things.

Harmony builds; discord destroys.

Polish proverb

5

DEVELOPING THE INDIVIDUAL

**'Three cobblers with their wits combined,
equal Zhuge Liang the master-mind.'**
***Chinese proverb** *

The generic role of *leader* indicates that as a leader you should have – within the context of the common purpose – a relationship with the group as a whole, as if it was an individual person. Sun Tzu advises generals to do just that:

> The skilful general directs his army as if it were a single man. He leaves it no choice but to obey . . .
> Deal with a whole army as if it were a single man. Apply them to their task . . .

And yet groups or teams of all sizes and shapes are always composed of individual persons, each with his or

* Zhuge was a famous statesman and strategist, chief minister of the state of Shu during the Three Kingdoms period, 220–280 CE.

her own unique set of needs. The wise leader meets these individual needs just as a parent does for his children. As Sun Tzu says,

> Regard your soldiers as your children, and they will follow you into the deepest valleys; look on them as your own beloved sons, and they will stand by you even unto death.

The story of the famous general Wu Ch'i illustrates the principle. According to one contemporary account:

> He wore the same clothes and ate the same food as the meanest of his soldiers, refused to have either a horse to ride or a mat to sleep on, carried his own surplus rations wrapped in a parcel, and shared every hardship with his men.
>
> One of his soldiers was suffering from an abscess, and Wu Ch'i himself sucked out the poisonous fluid. The soldier's mother, hearing this, began wailing and lamenting. Somebody asked her, saying, 'Why do you cry? Your son is only a common soldier, and yet the commander-in-chief himself has sucked out the poison from his sore.' The woman replied: 'Many years ago Lord Wu performed a similar service for my husband, who never left him afterwards, and finally met his death at the hands of the enemy. And now that he has done the same for my son, he too will fall fighting I know not where.'

As individuals, we respond to those who care for us – those who meet our individual needs. It is futile to expect individuals in any organization to respond by giving their best unless the organization – the leadership at all levels – demonstrates in the most practical way *that each individual matters*. In a large organization like an army, it is of course impossible that the strategic leader should personally care for each individual, although it is not unknown for soldiers to believe that is the case, and when that happens the effect is always powerful.

Notice that element of reciprocity in the story of Wu Ch'i. As Plutarch wrote in the first century CE, 'Evidence of trust begets trust, and love is reciprocated by love.' Sixteen centuries later, the English writer Richard Baxter observed: 'I saw that he that will be loved must love; and he that rather chooses to be more feared than loved, must expect to be hated, or loved but diminutively. And he that will have children, must be a father; and he that will be a tyrant must be content with slaves'.

The meeting of basic human needs – food, shelter, safety and other tangible conditions of service – is always the first priority when it comes to the third circle of leadership responsibility: *developing the individual*. Nowadays, a person's salary is the principal means by which they meet both their own individual needs and those of their families. Salary, incidentally, derives from *salarium*: money allowed to Roman soldiers for the purchase of salt. Leaders have a responsibility for ensuring that the wages their team members receive are fair, and that they are paid promptly at the appointed times.

As we are persons, however, we have a set of less material or tangible needs. They are more mental and spiritual in nature. For example, we all have a need – stronger in some than in others – to use our abilities in the service of others. We need to contribute.

Confucius was clearly in the business of helping his students to contribute to society as both good leaders and leaders for good. The young men who came to him were seeking education with a practical end in mind. Confucius, as a natural philosopher and lover of truth, may have held up to them the pursuit of goodness as an end in itself, for what philosopher would not? But, as he humorously remarked, he found few who loved virtue for its own sake:

> The Master said, 'I suppose I should give up hope. I have yet to meet the man who is as fond of virtues as he is of beauty in women.' (15:13)

Confucius was on surer ground when he saw his task as helping others to prepare themselves for public service. For in order to do so they needed to develop their potential – their abilities or talents – and that is where he felt most able to be of help. Nothing distressed Confucius more than a premature death of one of his students, robbing the world of a man of promise. Of one such student, Yen Yuan, he said: 'I watched him making progress, but I did not see him realize his capacity to the full. What a pity!' (9:21).

The general principle behind his attitude is that loving another person means you will want to bring out the best in them.

> The Master said, 'The gentleman helps others to realize what is good in them; he does not help them to realize what is bad in them. The small man does the opposite.' (12:16)

> The Master said, 'Can you love anyone without making him work hard? Can you do your best for anyone without educating him?' (14:7)

Confucius himself applied that principle to his educational work, but it is also applicable within the context of leadership. Here, however, there is a constraint: the developmental opportunities offered to an individual team member by a leader should enhance his or her present or future contribution to the common task. Here the work of the business leader differs from the leadership of a parent at home or a teacher in school.

In fact, and especially in the world of work, many of the ways a leader can develop individuals will be symbiotic. Effective delegation, for example, self-evidently serves the common task, but it also – if wisely done – develops the individual concerned. It kills two birds with one stone.

Another good example of this symbiosis occurs when a leader asks a team member – especially a junior one – for their suggestions. Listening to advice in this way improves decisions – remember the three cobblers at the head of this chapter, an example of the 'wisdom of crowds' in action. But consulting an individual acts as a form of recognition: as a leader you are showing the person that their opinion is valued, which means *they* are valued. Hence it meets individual needs.

Moreover, there is a principle that the more that people share in decisions that affect their working life, the more they will tend to be motivated to implement them. Listening generates commitment. Therefore a wise leader always regards his team as if they are equal partners with him in the common task. And that entails listening to each member in the way that the leader expects others to listen to him or her.

Alongside the Eastern and Western traditions of leadership stands the tribal tradition. Unlike its two counterparts, it has no geographical reference, for all modern non-Africans are descended from just a couple of thousand people, organized in clans or tribes, who left Africa between 50,000 and 20,000 years ago. We are all products of the tribal tradition shared by our distant but common ancestors; it informs our shared DNA, especially when it comes to expectations about leadership. The tribal chief is our archetypal leader.

What for many of us is a deeply buried geological stratum is for other societies very much on the surface, or just below it. This unevenness of social development brings with it the advantage that we can still study the archetypal leader, that shadowy figure who inhabits our human genes like a ghost.

Remember that the tribal leader had no police force. He could only get things done if free and equal tribesmen – especially the heads of families – shared in the decision and thus shared in commitment. And that could not happen unless he listened quietly and with patience to all that the key individuals had to say for or against some proposed course of action. No chief should be 'hard of hearing', as the ancient Ashanti people in what is now modern Ghana once reminded their newly elected king. They delivered the following ceremonial chant to their king during his instal-lation ceremony in the tribal capital of Kumasi:

Tell him that
We do not wish for greediness;
We do not wish that he should curse us;
We do not wish that his ears should be hard of
    hearing;
We do not wish that he should call people fools;
We do not wish that he should act on his own
    initiative;
We do not wish things done as in Kumasi;
We do not wish that it should ever be said 'I have no
    time, I have no time';

We do not wish personal abuse;
We do not wish personal violence

As a small boy, Nelson Mandela accompanied his father, a Thembu tribal chief, to the Great Place – a meeting place of the paramount chief in his palace in the tribal centre of Mqhekezweni. Here the tribal chiefs and any Thembus who wished to attend would meet to discuss their affairs. As would have been the case for the Ashanti in Kumasi, the paramount chief was surrounded by his councillors of high rank, who acted as both a senate and as a highest court of appeal. In recollecting this experience, Mandela could see with hindsight that it had had a formative influence on him:

> My later notions of leadership were profoundly influenced by observing the regent and his court. I watched and learned from the tribal meetings that were regularly held at the Great Place ... As a leader, I have always followed the principles I first saw demonstrated at the Great Place. I have always endeavoured to listen to what each and every person in a discussion had to say before venturing my own opinion. Oftentimes, my own opinion will simply represent a consensus of what I heard in the discussion.

We find Confucius advocating the same principle of consultation. Listen to others, he reiterates, even if they are lower down than you in the social hierarchy (5:15). Even if you are wise and knowledgeable, he advises, don't appear so to others in a way that deters them from offering you their opinions. Don't just go through the motions; genuinely listen to what others have to say and then weigh it in the balance of your mind.

> Tseng-Tzu said, 'To be able yet to ask the advice of those who are not able. To have many talents yet to ask the advice of those who have few. To have yet to appear to want. To be full yet to appear empty. To be transgressed against yet not mind. It was towards this end that my friend [Confucius] used to direct his efforts.' (8:5)

Confucius gives us an example of a lowly official in a planning meeting who asked a single question challenging the prevailing assumption. Like most people who don't speak unless they have something worth saying, and then say it succinctly, Min Tzu-ch'ien commanded a respectful hearing from his seniors – not least from Confucius:

> The people of Lu were rebuilding the treasury. Min Tzu-ch'ien said, 'Why not simply restore it? Why must it be totally rebuilt?'
> The Master said, 'Either this man does not speak or he says something to the point.' (11:14)

As Confucius came to know his ambitious young companions better, he noticed that many of them shared a particular tendency: they were very self-centred. In particular, they were preoccupied by what others thought about them, or, to be more precise, what others failed to think about them. Their considerable abilities, they kept saying, were being overlooked or ignored by others who should be promoting them on their merits. It was no wonder they had not received office in the first place, or promotion to the rank they deserved. It was not their fault – it was the fault of those who failed to recognize their talents.

Confucius constantly challenged this attitude. The right attitude for a leader, he countered, is to be other-centred, not self-centred:

> The Master said, 'It is not the failure of others to appreciate your abilities that should trouble you, but rather your failure to appreciate theirs.' (1:16)

> The Master said, 'The gentleman is troubled by his own lack of ability, not by the failure of others to appreciate him.' (15:19)

> The Master said, 'Do not worry because you have no official position. Worry about your qualifications. Do not worry because no one appreciates your abilities. Seek to be worthy of appreciation.' (4:14)

Stop being so anxious about what others think about you, Confucius is saying, and apply yourself to being worthy of their appreciation – whether it comes your way or not. Sharpen your scythe: be ready to lead.

Appreciating the abilities of others enables you as a leader to develop others by promoting them to positions of responsibility. But you cannot do so unless you have gauged accurately their ability.

> The Master said, 'Ming Kung-ch'uo would be more than adequate as steward to great noble families like Chao or Wei, but he would not be suitable as councillor even in a small state like T'eng or Hsüeh.' (14:11)

When it comes to judging people's ability as leaders, Confucius has no time for formal tests. Indeed, he dismisses in a sentence what sounds like a very early form of psychometric testing:

> Tzu-kung was given to grading people. The Master said, 'How superior he is! For my part I have no time for such things.' (14:29)

Yet, you may object, the abilities of some people are not all that easy to assess. Certainly that can be the case. The Japanese, for instance, talk of such a person as being like a *hira-andon*, a lamp seen in broad daylight.

The Confucian guiding principle for knowing people is essentially to judge them by their deeds, not their words. And others who speak with authority as leaders concur. 'The truth is,' wrote Napoleon in *Maxims* (1804–15), 'men are very hard to know; and yet, not to be deceived, we must judge them by their present actions, but for the present only'.

Not being self-preoccupied, a true leader is observant of others: he keeps his eyes and ears open. Therefore, over time, he acquires knowledge of others working over him, with him or under him: he can accurately predict how they will respond or how they will perform if given a certain kind of task. A leader with awareness, understanding and practice in observation will not find it so difficult to know others for his purposes, or so Confucius claims:

> The Master said, 'Look at the means a man employs, observe the path he takes and examine where he feels at home. In what way is a man's true character hidden from view?' (2:10)

> The Master said, 'In his errors a man is true to type. Observe the errors and you will know the man.' (14:7)

There will be, however, situations when a leader is in doubt about the wisdom of promoting a particular person. It is perhaps rather easier than Confucius allows to get it wrong. Even otherwise very good leaders often reveal weakness when it comes to decisions about people: they lack judgement in this department. It is their Achilles' heel – so-called from a legend that the goddess Thetis took her son Achilles by the heel and dipped him in the River Styx to make him invulnerable, but the heel in her hand remained dry; the hero was eventually slain by an arrow wound in his heel. And foolish appointments can only rebound like vicious boomerangs.

Yet any uncertainty about the ability of some potential candidates for promotion is no excuse, Confucius argues, for failing to promote those about whose merit there can be no argument. As for the good leaders you might have overlooked, don't worry about it: if real talent exists, it is sure to find a market:

> While he was steward to the Chi Family, Chung-kung asked about government. The Master said, 'Set an example for your officials to follow; show leniency towards minor offenders; and promote men of talent.'
>
> 'How does one recognize men of talent to promote?'
>
> The Master said, 'Promote those you do recognize. Do you suppose others will allow those you fail to recognize to be passed over?' (13:2)

KEY POINTS

- ☾ As a leader, you are responsible for task, team and individual. In the context of the shared common task, you should have a relation with the group as a whole – as if it is one person – but also a set of equal but different relations with each individual person in your team. Remember, you should have no favourites: all your ducks are swans.

◡ There are many ways of helping individuals within the frame of work – helping them, for example, to resolve a personal problem that is affecting their work – but Confucius focuses on two fundamentals: listen to many and promote the deserving few.

◡ Listening to individuals with ideas or suggestions meets a task need: it can significantly improve the quality of your decisions as a leader. But it also meets an individual person's need to be heard, to contribute and to be recognized. As the Chinese say, to be listened to with respect gives face to the person concerned.

◡ Where groups or individuals have been consulted before a decision, they are more likely to be committed and enthusiastic in implementing it. So take as much time as the situation allows to consult others before you make decisions.

◡ Part of the leader's role in regard to *developing the individual* – especially at operational and strategic levels – is to know the unique strengths of each member of their team, and to promote those with the necessary talent when opportunity arises. In order to know others in this way, however, you need to free yourself from self-preoccupied concern with your own personality or prospects.

ᴗ Make sure you promote those who merit it. If you inadvertently overlook a hidden talent in others, do not worry about it, for if real talent exists others will eventually promote the person concerned. Here, as elsewhere, the golden rule is to do your best.

If you wish to succeed, consult the people.

Chinese proverb

PART TWO

SOME QUALITIES
NECESSARY IN LEADERS

6

ENTHUSIASM

'The very life-blood of our enterprise'
William Shakespeare

Why is enthusiasm so important in a leader? A clue lies in the original Greek word *enthousiasmos*, which literally means to be possessed by a god, or – as we would say – to be inspired. Enthusiasm is contagious. Think about it. If you are not inspired yourself, how can you expect to inspire others?

To enthuse or inspire others, then, is to arouse in them an enthusiasm for the common purpose that matches your own. Admiral Lord Nelson (1758–1805) had a natural genius for this kind of leadership. After one successful action when Nelson was still a young captain, his commander-in-chief Admiral Lord St Vincent wrote him a letter which contains this compliment:

'I never saw a man in our profession who possessed the magic art of infusing the same spirit into others which inspire their own actions . . . all agree there is but one Nelson.'

Nelson never lost that infectious enthusiasm. As his lifelong friend and successor Admiral Collingwood said of him, 'He possessed the zeal of an enthusiast, directed by talents which Nature had very bountifully bestowed on him, and everything seemed, as if by enchantment, to prosper under his direction. But it was the effect of system, and nice combination [a coordinated and effective sequence of moves], not of chance.'

Confucius was also a lifelong enthusiast. In his case, it was primarily an enthusiasm for both study and for thinking things out for himself, coupled with a love of teaching others to do the same. 'At fifteen, I set my heart on learning', he tells us, and once that flame was lit, it burnt brightly all his days:

> The Master said, 'In a hamlet of ten households, there are bound to be those who are my equal in doing their best for others and in being trustworthy in what they say, but they are unlikely to be eager to learn as I am.' (5:28)

> The Master said, 'Quietly to store up knowledge in my mind, to learn without flagging, to teach without

growing weary, these present me with no difficulties.' (7:2)

The Governor of She asked Tzu-lu about Confucius. Tzu-lu did not answer him. The Master said, 'Why did you not simply say something to this effect: he is the sort of man who forgets to eat when he tries to solve a problem that has been driving him to distraction, who is so full of joy that he forgets his worries and who does not notice the onset of old age?' (7:19)

The Master said, 'To be fond of something is better than merely to know it, and to find joy in it is better than merely to be fond of it.' (6:20)

The kind of enthusiasm that Confucius had in mind is close to being wholehearted in what you are doing, so that you can give it your undivided attention. Conversely, a lack of enthusiasm in a group or organization may be symptomatic of being in two minds either about the proposed aim or the plan being pursued.

Wholeheartedness is the quality of being undivided in purpose, enthusiasm or will. Your actions will be performed with all possible effort and attention: you are wholly present in your work and to others working with you. A variant word in English is whole-souled: to be moved by ardent enthusiasm or single-minded devotion. It is the gift of having no reservations in mind about the business in hand. If you as a leader are stirred and moved in your whole being in this way, how can those working with you remain unaffected? You are no longer in two minds.

> The Master said, 'There are three things constantly on the lips of the gentleman, none of which I have succeeded in following: A man of benevolence never worries; a man of wisdom is never in two minds; a man of courage is never afraid.'
>
> Tzu-kung said, 'What the Master has just quoted is a description of himself.' (14:28)

The clearest statement from Confucius on the need for leaders to inspire enthusiasm in their people – and there-fore, by implication, to be enthusiastic themselves – comes in another conversation with his neighbour and friend, the chief minister of his own state of Lu.

> Chi K'ang Tzu asked, 'How can one inculcate in the common people the virtue of reverence, of doing their best and of enthusiasm?'
>
> The Master said, 'Rule over them with dignity and they will be reverent; treat them with kind-ness and they will do their best; raise the good and

instruct those who are backward and they will be imbued with enthusiasm.' (2:20)

It is the length of the journey that induces weariness and a flagging of spirits in many people. They lose their vision and their enthusiasm along the way. The best leaders, however, never give up; they remain whole-souled in the work at hand, however demanding. If they do feel the pace and the going is rough, they don't show it. Characteristically, they never think of retiring. As the American humorist Mark Twain once said: 'I have got nothing against retirement, as long as it doesn't interfere with my work.'

> Tzu-lu asked about government. The Master said, 'Encourage the people to work hard by setting an example of yourself.' Tzu-lu asked for more. The Master said, 'Do not allow your efforts to slacken.' (1:13)

> Tzu-chang asked about government. The Master said, 'Over daily routine do not show weariness, and when there is action to be taken, give of your best.' (14:12)

Notice how Confucius applies enthusiasm – sustained enthusiasm – even to the domain of daily routine, or – to widen the term – administration. For him, there is no divide between the work of a leader and a manager or administrator. If a manager of routine work shows enthusiasm and energy to the day's end, he is more than a manager – he is a leader. In the last century, various British and American writers used to make a sharp comparison between managers and leaders, mainly to the advantage of the latter. In doing so, however, they were unconsciously making what philosophers now call a 'category mistake'. An example of such a conceptual error is to treat *fruit* as if it was the same kind of word as *apples*, *bananas* or *plums*. You can eat the latter but you can't eat *fruit* – for it is an abstract or generic word covering all the different forms. Following that analogy, being a manager is just one of the many forms that the generic role of *leader* may take.

The best leaders always value good administration. They set an example by doing their share of it as well as they can. Moreover, they tend to value highly – and publicly – those team members of their organizations whose duties lie more at the 'daily routine' end of the spectrum of work. Doing this kind of administrative work, day in and day out, is vital for the survival and good name of the business. A true leader never allows one team member or group to look down upon another as doing inferior work: it may be different, but it is not inferior. Where would the brain surgeon be without the operating-theatre staff? Do you value the mechanics who service the aircraft you fly in less than the pilots who conduct you safely to your destination?

KEY POINTS

- The mere presence of a sound purpose is obviously not enough. It must be *felt* to be sound by all. In other words, it must be surcharged with a dynamic emotion, with a hopefulness, with an abounding, robust sense of joy in the job.

- Good leaders *are* enthusiasts. Can you think of any true leader you have met or read about who lacks enthusiasm?

- Enthusiasm is the quality in a leader that enables him to infuse others with the same spirit that animates himself.

- The human spirit is such that it is sometimes daunted by the enormity of a task or wearied by ceaseless daily demands or ground down by constant failure. We all need encouragement, not least those responsible for routine work or the more mundane administrative tasks. It is a function of a good leader to encourage others.

- As a leader, you should be able to draw upon deeper spiritual resources to sustain you to your journey's end. It is quite possible to be as enthusiastic about your work when you are writing the last chapter as you were upon the threshold of your career. Never

let others – however soul-destroying they may be
– rob you of your enthusiasm.

◗ 'When a man is eager and willing, the gods join in.'
So said the earliest great Greek dramatist Aeschylus,
a contemporary of Confucius.

◗ 'In everyone's life, at some time,' said Albert
Schweitzer, 'our inner fire gives out. It is then
burst into flames by an encounter with another
human being. We should be grateful for those
people who rekindle the inner spirit.' Should your
inner fire have burnt low, why not allow your
encounter with Confucius to rekindle the flames?

The pleasure of doing good is the only one that will
not wear out.

Chinese proverb

7

INTEGRITY

**'Trust being lost, all the social intercourse
of men is brought to naught.'**
Livy, Roman historian

Confucius is insistent upon the importance of trustworthiness in a leader, and he recognized that in order to inspire others' trust, a leader must have integrity.

> The Master said, 'Duke Wen of Chin was crafty and lacked integrity. Duke Huan of Ch'i, on the other hand, had integrity and was not crafty.' (14:15)

We can assume that Duke Wen was not acceptable to Confucius – how could he be? For integrity certainly implies, among other things, being trustworthy or reliable in word. It would not be an exaggeration to say that Confucius regards integrity as the linchpin of moral character; indeed, he uses that very metaphor:

The Master said, 'I do not see how a man can be acceptable who is untrustworthy in word. When a pin is missing in the yoke-bar of a large cart or in the collar-bar of a small cart, how can the cart be expected to go?' (2:22)

'Integrity without knowledge is weak and useless, and knowledge without integrity is dangerous and dreadful,' Dr Samuel Johnson once said. Clearly integrity on its own is never going to be enough: it is the foundation but not the actual house of leadership. By describing Duke Huan of Ch'i as 'not crafty', Confucius may have been paying him a compliment. Be that as it may, a leader needs both integrity and the quality of judgement that Greek contemporaries of Confucius called *phronesis*.

Translated into Latin as *prudentia* and thence into English as *prudence*, what *phronesis* really means is practical wisdom. Wisdom is impossible to define – you know it when you see it – but we can discern its chemical elements. It is an alchemist's blend of *intelligence, experience* and *goodness*, qualitatively different from mere craftiness or cunning. It enables you, as the Greeks would say, to do the right thing at the right time and in the right way. I don't have to tell you how important that ability is for a leader, be it in his dealings with task, team or individual.

A departmental minister or senior councillor, Confucius insists, also needs both integrity and practical wisdom – not to mention moral courage – if he is to render his lord true service.

Duke Ting asked, 'Is there such a thing as a single saying that can lead a state to prosperity?'

Confucius answered, 'A saying cannot quite do that. There is a saying among men: "It is difficult to be a ruler, and it is not easy to be a subject either." If the ruler understands the difficulty of being a ruler, then is this not almost a case of a saying leading the state to prosperity?'

'Is there such a thing as a saying that can lead the state to ruin?'

Confucius answered, 'A saying cannot quite do that. There is a saying among men: "I do not at all enjoy being a ruler, except for the fact that no one goes against what I say." If what he says is good and no one goes against him, good. But if what he says is not good and no one goes against him, then is this not almost a case of a saying leading the state to ruin?' (13:15)

That willingness to stand up to a powerful leader when he begins to lead in the wrong direction is the test of a minister's integrity, but it applies beyond the realm of government to all working contexts. All team members, associates or colleagues should be fearless in speaking the truth to their leaders if the occasion calls for it.

Tzu-lu asked about the way to serve a lord. The Master said, 'Make sure that you are not being dishonest with him when you stand up to him.' (14:22)

Today, a minister can choose to resign from his office in the government if the issue at stake threatens his personal and professional integrity. Apparently a similar option was open to ministers in China some 2,500 years ago:

> Chi Tzu-jan asked, 'Can Chung Yu and Jan Ch'iu be called great ministers?'
>
> The Master said, 'I had expected a somewhat different question. It never occurred to me that you were going to ask about Yu and Ch'iu. The term 'great minister' refers to those who serve their lord according to the Way and who, when this is no longer possible, relinquish office. Now men like Yu and Ch'iu can be described as ministers appointed to make up the numbers.'
>
> 'In that case, are they the kind that will always do as they are told?'
>
> 'No. They will not do so when it comes to patricide or regicide.' (11:24)

Clearly, Confucius doesn't award the two ministers in question, who he presumably knew well, the highest marks for either competence or integrity. They are placemen – not outstanding in any way. But, wanting to be truthful and fair about them, Confucius doesn't accept the suggestion that they are totally without integrity. They, too, have their basic sticking point: like all good people, there are things they could not bring themselves to do. Even if the alternative is torture and death at the hands of a tyrant, these two ministers would choose that rather than, say, kill their own fathers.

ↄↄcc

The primary meaning of integrity is wholeness or sound-ness. Integrity implies a unity – an interdependence of parts and completeness or perfection of the whole. But integrity also means adherence to a set of moral, artistic or other values, especially truth, that are – so to speak – outside oneself. And so integrity is closely related to an undeviating honesty in what you say or do. Therefore it is entirely incompatible with any form of insincerity. Consider the personal ideal that Mahatma Gandhi set before himself: 'What you think, what you say and what you do are in harmony.' It is a good star for all leaders to follow.

A person of integrity, then, is honest to such a degree that they are incapable of being false to a trust, responsi-bility or pledge – or to their own standards of conduct. For integrity is the opposite of a condition where a person can be moved by opportunist or self-seeking impulses, which threaten to break up his unity as a whole being.

For Confucius the foundation of any government is the trust of the people. He had the wisdom to see that this principle applied in all states, whatever their form of government. Ultimately, he perceived, any government depends upon the trust if not the consent of the people.

And, as Confucius tirelessly taught, rulers ignore this principle at their peril. However well a government provides for the protection of its people or for its sustenance, if it neglects the mutual trust between itself and its subjects, the very foundation of a civilized society is threatened.

> Tzu-kung asked about government. The Master said, 'Give them enough food, give them enough arms, and the common people will have trust in you.'
>
> Tzu-kung said, 'If one had to give up one of these three, which should one give up first?'
>
> 'Give up arms.'
>
> Tzu-kung said, 'If one had to give up one of the remaining two, which should one give up first?'
>
> 'Give up food. Death has always been with us since the beginning of time, but when there is no trust, the common people will have nothing to stand on.' (12:7)

Sticking to the right path, deviating neither to the left nor to the right, is a metaphor for integrity. Confucius often reread and reflected on the *Odes*. A revered collection of some three hundred poems already ancient in his day, the *Odes* marked the beginning of Chinese literature and served a function in China not unlike the Homeric poems in Greece, though they were very different in character. In Ode 297, which includes the description of a team of horses pulling a carriage and going straight ahead without swerving to left or right, he found what he believed to be the moral message of the whole anthology.

> The Master said, 'The *Odes* are three hundred in number. They can be summed up in one quotation: *Swerving not from the right path*.' (2:2)

A leader with integrity, the English poet William Words-worth wrote in his poem 'The Happy Warrior', is one:

> Who comprehends his trust, and to the same
> Keeps faithful, with singleness of aim;
> And therefore does not stop, nor lie in wait
> For wealth or honour, or for worldly state.

Such a person will be true to the highest principle he knows. He will never betray the truth or trifle with it; he will never make a decision from self-regarding motives; he will never yield to the persuasion of friends or the pressure of critics, unless either conforms to his own standards of right and wrong; he will face the consequences of his attitudes, decisions and actions, however costly they may be; and he will not be loud in self-justification, but quietly confident and humbly ready to explain.

Political leaders with integrity shine like stars in their generation, however dark the sky may be. Of Joseph Addison

LUCAN
LIBRARY
TEL. 6216422

(1672–1719), for example, who held political office, his friend and fellow poet Alexander Pope could write:

> Statesman, yet friend to truth; of soul sincere,
> In action faithful, and in honour clear;
> Who broke no promise, serv'd no private end,
> Who gain'd no title, and who lost no friend.

Ambition, in its original undesirable sense as an inordinate striving after rank and wealth, always tests one's integrity. Yet those who sacrifice their integrity upon the altar of ambition may well live to regret it bitterly. As a Chinese proverb expresses it: *He who sacrifices his integrity to achieve his ambition burns a picture to obtain the ashes.*

Because integrity is so integral to being a person, and because the vast majority of people are good, it is always best to assume that others are persons of integrity until they supply you with evidence to the contrary. Yet how do you combine this trusting attitude with a realistic assessment of people you encounter? Confucius is particularly good on this point:

> The Master said, 'Is a man not superior who, without anticipating attempts at deception or presuming acts of bad faith, is, nevertheless, the first to be aware of such behaviour?' (14:31)

The advantage of taking others on trust in this way is that it tends to bring out the best in them, and that is precisely what a love of people – as a general moral principle – demands. For trust is halfway to love. Yes, if you trust others you will be let down sometimes, for even a vigilant person may be taken by surprise. But, as Samuel Johnson once commented to a friend, 'It is happier to be sometimes cheated than not to trust.'

Lao-tzu also points out how our natural reciprocity may work in our favour: if you trust a person, they will tend to return your trust. Conversely, if you mistrust others, they in turn will tend to mistrust you:

> Those who are good I treat as good. Those who are not good I also treat as good. In so doing I gain in goodness. Those who are of good faith I have faith in. Those who are lacking in good faith I also have faith in. In so doing I gain in good faith. (49:111)

People must be able to trust their leaders. They want to feel that their interests are safe in their leader's hands – that he will not betray them, or sell out, or get tired of serving them and start putting self-interest first. They want to feel a sense of solidity, of honesty, of reliability. 'We can trust him' and 'he does not lie to us' and 'he keeps his promises' are tributes he must have earned. In short, they want the leader to possess integrity.

KEY POINTS

- In leadership, example is everything. As the Moorish proverb says: *When the shepherd is corrupt, so is his flock.*

- Integrity implies such rectitude that one is incorruptible or incapable of being false to a trust, a responsibility or one's own standards. As the Latin proverb says: *Integrity is the noblest possession.*

- There can be no confidence without truth. If you want to lose the confidence of your team, try any of the following behaviours: dishonesty, duplicity, deceitfulness, lying, dissimulation or manipulation.

- What do men gain by telling lies? Aristotle answered his own question: 'When they speak truth, they are not believed.'

- Those occupying leadership roles who completely lack integrity are what we call 'blind shepherds'. They are not really 'bad' leaders, because they are not leaders at all: they are *misleaders*. Woe to the people afflicted with them! As an ancient Hebrew proverb says: *When God wants to punish the sheep he sends them a blind shepherd.*

- 'It is an old adage that honesty is the best policy. This applies to public as well as private life, to states as well as individuals.' So wrote George Washington (1732–99), in a letter to James Madison. Is honesty the policy of your nation or your organization? Is it *your* policy as a leader?

☻ The Master said, 'Make it your guiding principle to do your best for others and to be trustworthy in what you say.' (9:25)

Trust, like the soul, once gone is gone for ever.
(Catullus, Roman poet, c. 84–54 BCE)

8

TOUGH AND DEMANDING BUT FAIR

'To others a heart of love;
to himself a heart of steel'
St Augustine

True leaders are tough and demanding but fair. They are not easily satisfied. Confucius captures this quality in one of his classic principles: *The best leader is easy to serve and difficult to please.* (13:25)

Leadership is not about popularity as such; it all depends upon the grounds for it. For popularity – being liked – should not be taken at face value.

> Tzu-kung asked, ' "All in the village like him." What do you think of that?'
> The Master said, 'That is not enough.'
> ' "All in the village dislike him." What do you think of that?'
> The Master said, 'That is not enough either.

119

"Those in his village who are good like him and those who are bad dislike him." That would be better.'

The Master said, 'Be sure to go carefully into the case of the man who is disliked by the multitude. Be sure to go carefully into the case of the man who is liked by the multitude.' (15:28)

Toughness as a quality in a person suggests a strength coming from an inner spirit that is firm and unyielding, able to resist effectively any attempts to destroy or over-come it. The word carries, however, an implication of flexibility, like tempered steel or a tree bending in the wind, rather than the hardness or solidity of concrete. Toughness should result in a tenacity that means you are persistent, but not by always resorting to the same method.

The quality of being demanding may not fit some people's idea of the modern leader, for a demand is literally an insistent or peremptory request, made out of a sense of entitlement.

But, if you think about it, the role of leader does confer upon you the authority to make demands, providing of course they fall within your terms of reference. Do you make enough use of this prerogative?

Please don't misunderstand me here. There is a vast difference between issuing a military-style order or com-mand – like 'Right turn!' – and making a leadership demand. For more often than not a demand is couched in the form of a question or request. There is usually no need for a raised voice or peremptory tone. If it is something that the other person is clearly expected to do – and they know it – then you are making a demand. If the other person goes away unaware of that clear expectation, then you have failed to communicate effectively.

It is said that the senate of ancient Rome had *auctoritas* but not *potestas*. In other words, their directives had more than the force of a request but less than the force of a command. Most leadership demands fall within this broad spectrum.

There are three forms of authority in human affairs which should intertwine like three strands in a rope: the authority of position or office (the Roman *potestas*), the authority of knowledge and the authority of personality (sometimes called charisma).

In order to get free and equal people to cooperate and to achieve great things together, it is necessary today to draw upon the second and third forms of authority and not just upon the first. Positional authority is still important, but it is only one strand of the three-stranded rope. And it is unwise when climbing a mountain to entrust your life to a one-stranded rope. The art of leadership is using this blended authority to get things done without having to issue too many direct commands.

The Master said, 'If a man is correct in his own person, then there will be obedience without orders being given; but if he is not correct in his own person, there will not be obedience even though orders are given.' (13:6)

Confucius' phrase of being 'correct in his own person' may be interpreted today as signifying that he possesses the generic skills and qualities of leadership, such as integrity, fairness and being a good example. Shakespeare, who, like Confucius, largely discusses leadership in terms of the office of a king, offers us a list of twelve such qualities:

The king-becoming graces,
As justice, verity [integrity], temperance, stableness,
Bounty [generosity], perseverance, mercy, lowliness
    [humility],
Devotion, patience, courage, fortitude.

Such qualities contribute to a leader's personal authority. To this kind of authority, however, we should add the authority of knowledge – for, as the modern adage goes: *Authority flows to the one who knows.* A leader who knows his business is much more likely to be obeyed willingly than one who doesn't.

Those who occupy positions or offices of leadership who are not actually leaders – who lack both the forms of authority I have just outlined – can get things done only by exercising the authority of their office. Without the respect that a three-stranded rope of authority invariably brings, obedience will be tardy, to say the least. Shake-speare's king Macbeth is certainly not 'correct in his own person'. Angus observes of Macbeth to a companion:

Those he commands move only in command,
Nothing in love.

Before you go around being tough and demanding with others in the context of the common purpose, there is a necessary condition that has to be fulfilled.

The Master said, 'If one sets strict standards for one-self and makes allowances for others when making demands on them, one will stay clear of ill will.' (15:15)

In other words, if you are making demands on others, they will only respond willingly if you are not asking from them more than you ask from yourself. If, in St Augustine's words, you first act with a 'heart of steel' to yourself, then you can make demands on others without fearing any loss of goodwill on their part.

You can begin to see now what kind of a leader Confucius had in mind. The true leader goes ahead and shows the way, expecting others to accompany him on the journey. Yet he is fair when it comes to judging the performance or contribution of others, making allowances where they are justifiable but also rejecting reasons that are lame excuses in disguise.

The Master said, 'The gentleman is easy to serve but difficult to please. He will not be pleased unless you try to please him by following the Way, but when it comes to employing the services of others, he does so within the limits of their capacity.

'The small man is difficult to serve but easy to please. He will be pleased even though you try to please him by not following the Way, but when it comes to employing the services of others, he demands all-round perfection.' (13:25)

The 'small man' – the non-leader in a position of authority – who unreasonably demands all-round perfection in others clearly lacks knowledge of human nature. For, as the Japanese say: *Only he who knows his own weakness can endure those of others.*

One aspect of being tough and demanding is that you should be economical with praise. A constant flow of praise suggests that you are too easy to please, and people will tend to discount what you say. 'Praise,' said Samuel Johnson, 'like gold and diamonds, owes its value only to its scarcity.'

The great conductor Otto Klemperer expected the best from his players and didn't go into raptures when he got it. After one performance, however, he was so pleased with the orchestra that he looked at them and said, 'Good!' Overwhelmed, the musicians burst into applause. 'Not *that* good,' Klemperer said.

This story illustrates another aspect of praise: it matters who the person is who is giving it. A Roman proverb expresses this truth thus: *It is the greatest possible praise to be praised by a man who is himself deserving of praise.*

In order for a leader to be tough and demanding when the occasion demands, it is necessary for there to be a social distance – maintained by both parties – between leader and team. That doesn't imply a lack of friendliness on both sides: the real enemy is familiarity. There is some truth in the old proverb: *Familiarity breeds contempt.*

As the word suggests, familiarity reflects what goes on in family life, where long-continued association makes for freedom, informality, ease of address, and even the taking of some liberties. Outside that context, a stranger who is being familiar with you is assuming or claiming this kind of freedom and ease of address; they are acting as if they are members of your family, or close friends who have the status of being family.

The Master said, 'In one household, it is the women and the small men that are difficult to deal with. If you let them get too close, they become insolent. If you keep them at a distance, they complain.' (17:25)

Leaders have to strike that same balance. At one level, they are team members like everyone else. At another level, however, they are in the group but not of it.

Striking the inner balance between being too distant from people and being too close to them, between toughness and warmth, has its outward counterpart in the appearance of the leader, especially his face. Here Confucius set the standard for his students:

'The gentleman never dare neglect his manners whether he be dealing with the many or the few, the young or the old. Is this not being casual without being arrogant? The gentleman, with his robe and cap adjusted properly and dignified in his gaze, has a presence which inspires people who see him with awe. Is this not being awe-inspiring without appearing fierce?' (20:2)

The Master is cordial yet stern, awe-inspiring yet not fierce, and respectful yet at ease. (7:38)

This is how you too should look, Confucius told them, when you become leaders. It is a bearing that combines dignity – the Romans called it *gravitas* – with humanity.

As aspiring leaders, Confucius' students did their best to look like the Master, who was 'affable but dignified' (7:37). At first each of them could only copy one of the attributes they saw on his face, and not always the same one! But they were taking it step by step and going in the right direction, so Confucius was pleased.

> When in attendance on the Master, Min Tzu looked respectful and upright; Tzu-lu looked unbending; Jan Yu and Tzu-kung looked affable. The Master was happy. (11:13)

With or without robes of office or other outward symbols, a leader should always have a commanding presence. That refers to a power to impress one's personality on others, or to attract their attention, interest or admiration. It doesn't mean that you should talk more than others or more loudly, still less that you should draw attention to yourself. Quiet leaders can have great presence. After all, the tiger doesn't need to proclaim its tigritude.

In employing the services of others, a leader should always be just or fair. For justice in its different forms is a moral concept; it is the impersonal foundation of good personal relations. Confucius is quite clear about this requirement in a leader:

> The Master said of Tzu-ch'an that he had the way of the gentleman on four counts: he was respectful in the manner he conducted himself; he was reverent in the service of his lord, in caring for the common people, he was generous, and in employing their services, he was just. (5:16)

Confucius offers no definition of justice. Doubtless he believed that on earth it reflects the Way of Heaven, which is impartial in its dealings with men. Lao-tzu expressed this same idea thus:

> It is the way of heaven to show no favouritism.
> It is for ever on the side of the good man. (79:190)

In the context of a small team or larger organization, if you are in the role of leader, you should have no favourites. For if you specially favour one person over another, it creates discontent and disunity in the group. The Tsonga people in Africa have a wise saying: *The chief has no relatives.*

To be tough and demanding but fair is not the easiest or most pleasant aspect of being a leader. But this combination of qualities is essential, for as a result a leader will gain and retain respect, that necessary condition of leadership. So steel yourself to the task and make sure that in this context you do not fall short of what others expect of you. As an Italian proverb says: *By asking the impossible, you get the best possible.*

This may sound unreasonable, but, as George Bernard Shaw once remarked, 'Nothing is ever accomplished by a reasonable man.' Jan Leschly, then chief executive of one of the largest pharmaceutical companies in the world, once explained clearly what 'unreasonable' means in this context. 'If I think about my own life,' he said, 'the real big changes where I really learnt something, that was done by an unreasonable leader. I am not talking about being rude, about being nasty, about being unpleasant. I'm talking about unreasonable – asking for things that people say: "That's nearly impossible for us to do."'

'Many people die with their music still in them,' writes Oliver Wendell Holmes. As it is the function of the conductor to draw great music from the orchestra, so a leader's task is to evoke the talents of each player in the team.

> If, however, you are indulgent, but unable to make your authority felt; kind-hearted but unable to enforce your commands; and incapable, moreover, of quelling disorder: then your soldiers must be likened to spoilt children; they are useless for any practical purpose.
>
> *Sun Tzu, The Art of War*

KEY POINTS

- *No strength within, no respect without.* To be a leader you need the capacity to be tough and demanding but fair.

- A leader should not set out to be popular nor even to be liked, though of course, it is unnatural to enjoy not being liked. Respect attends leaders who know their business, and affection usually flows in its train.

- Be ruthless with yourself, never sparing yourself in the common cause, and others will respond willingly to your demands. Example is contagious.

- Demanding though he may be, the leader respects the other – the team or individual – as an equal. The other is always free to leave.

- The leader is there primarily to enable all to achieve the common task, however uphill the road. But in working with individuals, the good leader may be more a coach and consultant, even sometimes a mentor. Thereby a leader may often be the catalyst whereby others realize and bring unsuspected or hidden talents to market.

- As a leader you should be *easy to serve but hard to please.* Write these words of Confucius on your heart. Don't compromise your values or standards. Demand the very best from your team, and reward those who give it.

ɔ The faithful and prompt fulfilment of contractual obligations, such as the payment of wages, is the foundation of good relations at work. In personal relations, an impersonal relation is necessarily included and subordinated. Justice is the first expression of love.

The task of leadership is not to put greatness into people but to elicit it, because the greatness is there already.

John Buchan

9

WARMTH

**'Cold tea or rice is bearable,
but not cold looks or words.'**
Chinese proverb

To be warm implies a capacity for both feeling and express-
ing love, affection or interest, and doing so with depth,
ardour or fervency. A warm-hearted person tends to be
generous, unselfish and compassionate.

A warm-hearted man himself, genial and kindly by
nature, Confucius regarded warmth as an essential leadership quality. Why? In brief, because he believed that leaders
should exemplify the human quality of goodness. Love is
goodness in action. And could love be love if it lacked
warmth? Cold fish do not make good leaders.

Let me take you now deeper into the argument, not
least because it is so fundamentally important for how we
think about leadership today.

There is a fundamental principle of leadership that I have not shared with you before now: *leaders tend to reflect, exemplify or personify the qualities that are expected or required in their working groups.*

Take courage, for example. Courage doesn't make you a military leader. There are plenty of soldiers with courage – Shakespeare calls it 'the soldier's virtue' – who are not leaders. But you cannot be a leader of soldiers if your level of courage is, shall we say, below average. The spectacle of a group of soldiers having to persuade their officer to lead them from in front is not an attractive one, nor should it ever be necessary. As the Ugandan proverb says: *The one nearest the enemy is the real leader.*

This principle can be applied in all fields of human enterprise – leading teachers, nurses, researchers, actors, musicians, engineers and so on. How can you lead a team of nurses if you lack warmth, compassion or high professional standards?

Confucius takes this principle to a deeper and more universal level. How can you lead people, he asks, unless you yourself are a person – and an exemplary person at that? Let us consider what it means to be a person.

Confucius, ever alive to his surroundings and observant, is aware that there is a commonality about human nature. He believes, for example, that the Nine Nations – the barbaric ethnic tribal groups on China's borders – will respond to

moral example if presented with it (9:14). He adheres to
the principle that our common identity is essential, our
differences are accidental.

Confucius, however, lacked a key concept that is
needed in order to understand the common dimension
that binds human beings together. In fact, the idea was
being developed during his lifetime – and it was being
done at some distance away, in far-off Italy.

The dominant people in northern Italy – Etruria, as it
was then known – adopted from the Greeks the cult of
Dionysus, son of Zeus. Originally a god of the fertility of
nature, associated with wild and ecstatic religious rites, in
later traditions Dionysus is the god of wine who loosens
inhibitions and inspires creativity in music and poetry.
Plays were performed in his honour at his festival, each
actor wearing a distinctive mask known in Greek as a
prosopon. The Etruscan term for the mask was *phersu*; the
Romans adopted the word, changing it into *persona*, and it
migrated to the English language as *person*.

There are three elements that together make up the
concept of being a *person*: legal, social and – for want of a
better word – significance.

Being a *persona* in Rome meant that you had legal rights
and obligations, that you existed as far as Roman law was
concerned. Those not accorded that status, such as slaves
or children, were at the mercy of master or father. Indeed,
a *pater familias*, the head of a household, had the power to
put to death a rebellious son as well as a mutinous slave.

From that tiny seed in Roman law has grown our

modern and near-universal concept of human rights: that the existence of each person, irrespective of nation, age or gender, is recognized in international law. The second sentence of the preamble to the United Nations Charter, published in 1947, sets out as one of the principal aims of the new body: 'to reaffirm faith in human rights'.

The second element of the concept of *person* springs from the word's origins in drama. Being a person is not quite the same as being an individual. The actor plays his part – his *persona* – only in relation to the other actors in the play. Being a person, then, is a social concept. It is well expressed by the Bantu term *ubuntu*, much quoted by Nelson Mandela, which translates as 'I am a person because of other persons'. An African proverb makes a similar point: *It takes a whole village to raise a child.*

How did the notion of merely being a person come to carry with it a sense of weight or importance? Again, the seeds go back to Etruria in the age of Confucius. For the masks worn by the relatively few actors in the plays depicted gods or heroes. Consequently the Greeks and Romans used their 'mask' word *prosopon* or *persona* for someone of rank, note or distinction – what in English we would now call a personage. It is as if some property of the mask had rubbed off on the face of the wearer.

Therefore when the Greek New Testament tells us more than once that 'God is no respecter of persons' (*prosopon*), it means that an individual's rank or importance do not influence his judgement or come into the picture. The implication is that all persons are 'equal in the sight of God'; we are all significant by virtue of simply being persons. Significance here refers to a quality or character that should mark a person or thing as important, but that is not self-evident and may or may not be recognized.

Once again, the Charter of the United Nations is evidence that the world is now coming to accept this third element of personhood: the property of being a person. The sentence I have already quoted from continues: '... *to reaffirm faith in human rights, the dignity and worth of the human person*'.

Those who commit genocide or other crimes against people first have to strip their intended victims of their personhood; they are reduced in their eyes to being *Unter-menschen*, a borrowed word that literally means non-persons in the original German. A Chinese proverb makes the same point: *When a cat wants to eat its own kittens, it first declares them to be mice.* People can be stripped naked of their clothes by tyrants and their henchmen, but they cannot be divested of their dignity and worth as persons. It is the perpetrators of these terrible crimes against humanity who thereby lose their dignity and personhood; it is they who stand naked in Heaven's court.

⤳ↄↄcc⤲

Our state or condition of being persons is the necessary condition for the greatest and most distinctive thing in our lives – love. To the existential mystery of being a person is added the joyful mystery of being able to experience love.

> Fan Ch'ih asked about benevolence. The Master said, 'Love your fellow men.'
>
> He asked about wisdom. The Master said, 'Know your fellow men' (12:22)

Just to be clear, Confucius is not telling us that we should love all our fellow men equally, as if they are members of our family or close friends. We are men, not gods. Confucius is fully aware that the radiant warmth of the human heart varies in relation to social distance. Each person, however, needs to be given their due. There is no other human being who, in the Confucian tradition, can be treated entirely without love.

In the *Analects*, as the days go by, Confucius often smiles. A smile is the natural expression of warmth on the human face. It is difficult to fake; most people can tell the difference between a genuine smile and a false one. You can manoeuvre the twenty-two muscles in your face to produce a grin, but a genuine smile begins always in your eyes – like a light coming from within you.

> Tzu-hsia asked about being filial. The Master said, 'What is difficult to manage is the expression on one's face. As for the young taking on the burden when there is work to be done or letting the old enjoy the

wine and the food when these are available, that hardly deserves to be called filial.' (1:8)

Being unable to recognize the expressions on people's faces, Confucius adds elsewhere, is a form of social blindness (16:6).

Warmth towards others goes hand in hand with respect for persons. In the case of Confucius, it is a respect almost bordering on reverence. He admired those who never lost their reverence for persons even in the company of family or close friends:

> The Master said, 'Yen P'ing-chung excelled in friend-ship: even after long acquaintance he treated his friends with reverence.' (00:17)

What does it mean to treat another person with reverence? Confucius on one occasion gave his young companions a kind of demonstration. Just to set the scene, in his day the profession of musician was reserved for blind people – a remarkably civilized way of providing employment for a disabled group, given that Confucius lived 2,500 years ago.

> Mien, the Master Musician, called. When he came to the steps, the Master said, 'You have reached the

steps,' and when he came to the mat, the Master said, 'You have reached the mat.' When everyone was seated, the Master told him, 'This is So-and-so and that is So-and-so over there.'

After the Master Musician had gone, Tzu-chang asked, 'Is that the way to talk to a musician?' The Master said, 'Yes. That is the way to assist a musician.' (15:42)

In ancient China, as in our world today, some people occupying positions of authority regarded themselves – consciously or unconsciously – as above the law of love. In the West, the writings of Machiavelli (1469–1527) were sometimes cited by such rulers to justify their stance. For Machiavelli, statecraft centred upon a very different purpose of governing than the one envisaged by Confucius: not so much the good of the people, but more the acquisition and retention of power. In order to secure political ends, it was legitimate for princes to resort to means that no personal morality could justify. The shadow of Machiavelli falls across the great tyrants of the twentieth century such as Hitler and Stalin.

Tolstoy puts his finger on the cause of our problem in his last great novel, *The Resurrection* (1899). The hero Nekhlyudov is being conducted to the prison camps of distant Siberia. On the way he experiences the daily cruelty of officials and guards. Why, he asks himself, do men treat their fellow human beings in this inhuman way? Then the light dawns. It is only when they are occupying *roles*, he thinks, that they feel that they can behave in this cold, brutal way. Outside their roles, Tolstoy believes, they are doubtless normal, decent family men. Similarly, a Nazi concentration-camp guard might spend all day exterminating people in the gas chambers and then go home and read his children a bedtime story.

But in a moment of revelation Tolstoy's hero sees that there *are* no roles on earth that give licence for one person to degrade or humiliate others, or to inflict cruelty upon them.

'It all comes from the fact that men think there are circumstances when they may treat their fellow beings without love, but no such circumstances ever exist. Inanimate objects may be dealt with without love: you can cut down trees, make bricks, and hammer iron without love. But human beings cannot be treated without love – just as bees cannot be handled without care. That is the nature of bees. If you handle bees carelessly you will harm the bees and yourself as well. It is just the same with men. And this cannot be otherwise, for mutual love is the fundamental law of human life.

It is true that a man cannot force himself to love as he can force himself to work, but it does not follow that men may be treated without love, especially if something is required from them. If you feel no love for men – leave them alone. Occupy yourself with things, with your own self, with anything you please – but not with men.'

KEY POINTS

- *A leader should exemplify or personify the qualities expected, required and admired in their working groups.* By the same principle taken to a deeper level, he should exemplify the qualities of being a person.

- Our individual personalities are mixtures of good and bad, but humanity as a whole is predominately good. *A universal leader, then, will be a person who exemplifies such distinctively human qualities as goodness, kindness, humaneness and compassion.*

- Conversely, it is impossible for a bad or evil person to be a leader. He may, however, become a misleader and, upon seizing power, even become a tyrant.

- You can tell what kind of person someone is by the way they treat strangers.

- 'We cannot live only for ourselves,' wrote Herman Melville. 'A thousand fibres connect us with our fellow men; and among these fibres, as sympathetic threads, our actions run as causes, and they come back to us as effect.'

People always know somewhere inside them if they are loved. No gesture, talk, conciliation or pronouncements can prevail over that deep instinctive knowledge.

When leaders are worthy of respect, the people are willing to work for them. When their virtue is worthy of admiration, their authority can be established.

Huainanzi (Chinese philosopher, 4th century BCE)

10

HUMILITY

'In peace there's nothing so becomes a man
As modest stillness and humility.'
William Shakespeare

Referring to his favourite role model of a good ruler, the gifted Duke of Chou, Confucius said that 'if he was arrogant and miserly, then the rest of his qualities would not be worthy of admiration' (8:11). Why is arrogance such a disqualification for leadership? Why is it such an impairment of what it means to be a good person?

The word arrogance originates in the Latin verb *arrogare*, which means to claim for oneself. Thus an arrogant man is disposed to claim for himself – often in an overbearing or domineering manner – more consideration of importance than is justly warranted.

The Master said, 'Claims made immodestly are difficult to live up to.' (14:20)

The English describe someone who acts above themselves in this conceited and over-confident way as being *too big for his boots*.

> The Master said, 'The gentleman is at ease without being arrogant; the small man is arrogant without being at ease.' (13:26)

An absence of arrogance is a good working definition of humility. And to be without even the slightest toxic trace of spiritual pride is to be truly humble or 'lowly in spirit'.

Confucius values those who are in high positions of leadership and yet are self-effacing in manner or behaviour. He likes modest men. He noticed an example of such behaviour that pleased him while observing an armed struggle during a city siege: an officer who bravely stayed behind to protect his fellows but pretended that he had no choice.

> The Master said, 'Meng Chih Fan was not given to boasting. When the army was routed, he stayed in the rear. But on entering the gate, he goaded his horse on, saying, "I did not lag behind out of presumption. It was simply that my horse refused to go forward."' (6:15)

As I mentioned earlier, when people join together in teamwork there is – or should be – a tacit agreement that each member will set aside any desire for personal prominence at the expense of others. The team has become, as it were, a corporate person, one with its own group personality, and individual egos are laid aside by its members, like shoes on entering a temple.

In the Eastern tradition of leadership, the person who is in the role of *leader* is also bound by this convention. For, different as their role may be from the parts played by other team members, they are still primarily members of the team.

A leader imbued with the Eastern spirit, then, will not seek any special notice, honour or reward: he will not attempt to stand out from the others. Those coming from the more individualistic Western tradition, however, where the leader often acts as if he is entitled to take the lion's share of virtually everything (except, of course, failure!), the self-effacement of Eastern-style leaders can seem rather strange. Frederick T. Jane, for example, during a visit to Japan to collect materials for his book *The Imperial Japanese Navy*, happened to meet some veterans who had taken part in a daring torpedo attack on the enemy fleet in a battle at sea some five years previously. In his book, published in 1904, Jane shares with us a conversation he had with one of the officers in command on that famous day:

No Japanese officer who participated will tell you his share. I once met one of these, and asked him about the famous action.

147

'Oh yes,' said he, 'I was there. It was a very cold night.' Subsequently I learnt from another officer that this particular one had commanded the boat that sank the enemy flagship.

'But,' added my informant, 'he would not tell you and you should not ask. All did well; some were lucky, some were not. Since all did well they agreed not to speak of it after, and say who did this and who did that, for all are equally worthy of praise.'

The best of leaders, however, have always followed the Eastern model, perceiving themselves first and foremost as team members and putting the team – not their egos – centre stage. Group Captain Leonard Cheshire (1917–92), for example, who was awarded the Victoria Cross – Britain's highest award for gallantry – as a bomber pilot in the Second World War and who then went on to found the Cheshire Foundation Homes for the severely disabled, captured this spirit in a sentence:

Leaders there have to be, and these may appear to rise above their fellow men, but in their hearts they know only too well that what has been attributed to them is in fact the achievement of the team to which they belong.

It was not my good fortune to meet Leonard Cheshire in person, but I did briefly work in a team with John Hunt as our leader. Another former military man, Hunt also became a successful leader in peacetime. Today he is chiefly remembered for being the leader of the first expedition to conquer Mount Everest in 1953. This is what he has to say on the subject of leadership.

> In its true sense, leadership should mean *giving a lead by example*, even without a position of authority. True leadership is simply an expression of human greatness. Some of the finest examples of this aspect of leadership are displayed by men who have *no high position or reputation at stake*, but with much to lose in security, in comradeship and convenience, who stand up for what they know, from their conscience, to be right.

Knowing of my interest in leadership, John Hunt sent me the full source from which this quotation is taken. It was a lecture that he gave at an army cadet training centre in 1959, entitled 'Leadership in the Modern Age'. It is a rare example of a true leader capturing the essence of the art of leadership in plain and simple English, and it deserves not to be forgotten.

> Firstly, I will give you my definition of leadership, as applied to someone to whom other people are entrusted. To me, it is best described as the art of inspiring others to give of their best, and the courage to use this art. That is what leadership means to me: it demands that the leader operates from inside his

group, not from above it; that in setting a good example, he does not steal the initiative of the others; in other words, that he takes his full share – but no more than his share – of the job in hand.

This implies a willingness not merely to decentralize, or apportion the burden, but an ability to persuade each other member of the group that his is an equally essential job, and that each has his own liberty as well as responsibility to develop that part as a whole.

Good leadership derives from a right attitude to the job of leading; that this is only one of the jobs to be done. A leader has been well described as a 'first companion'. Then, of course, it is the art of blending the efforts of everyone concerned to produce a combined result.

Notice that Hunt sees leadership as 'only one of the jobs to be done'. The team leader, however large the team may be, is the first companion or associate: what the ancient Romans called a *primus inter pares* – first among equals.

Arrogance rests upon a foundation of sand: making presumptuous, unjustifiable or unsustainable claims about oneself, especially about one's relative importance in the scheme of things. These claims may not be conscious –

they seldom are. A person may therefore be arrogant without ever knowing it.

As a Moroccan proverb says: *The arrogant man has no friends.* Arrogance in any team member can be extremely divisive, and all the more so if he is in a leadership role. It goes against the grain of one of the three greater functions: *building and maintaining the team.*

But arrogance in a leader also threatens the general function of *achieving the task* as well. For a leader has higher positional power than other team members when it comes to making decisions. Effective decision-making depends on having good judgement. And good judgement in turn rests upon truth.

But an arrogant person does not see the truth about himself, and may vastly exaggerate his own powers of intuition or knowledge. They may believe their minds are much greater than those of others around them, whom they tend to despise. Therefore they see no need to consult with colleagues – still less subordinates – before making a decision: it is as if, in a god-like way, they always know best. Such men regard asking for advice as a confession of weakness.

You can see just how dangerous an arrogant person in a position of authority can be. The chances that he will prove to be a misleader are greatly increased.

A true leader should be a person of intellectual humility. By example and precept Confucius sets out the tent poles of intellectual humility, beginning with its most basic principle:

The Master said, 'Yu, shall I tell you what it is to know.
To say you know when you know, and to say you do
not when you do not, that is knowledge.' (17:2)

The Delphic Oracle once pronounced Socrates, the great
Greek philosopher of Athens (*c.* 470–399 BCE), as the wisest
man in Greece. Socrates humbly replied: 'It is because I
alone of all the Greeks know that I know nothing.'

Even if you do happen to be knowledgeable or wise, it
is best not to show it, or indeed to count on yourself as
such, as Lao-tzu suggests:

To know yet to think that one does not know is best;
Not to know yet to think that one knows will lead to
    difficulty.
It is by being alive to difficulty that one can avoid it.
The sage meets with no difficulty. It is because he is
    alive to it that he meets with no difficulty. (71:173)

Humility is not to be confused with any form of self-
deprecation: it is not about denigrating oneself. As Dag
Hammarskjöld, former Secretary-General of the United
Nations, said, 'Humility is just as much the opposite of
self-abasement as it is of self-exaltation.' It is the gift of
seeing oneself truthfully, and therefore seeing oneself in the
right relation to everything else. In other words, you see all
things, including your own role and contribution, in due
proportion.

'I believe the first test of a truly great man is his

humility,' writes John Ruskin in *Modern Painters*. 'I do not mean, by humility, doubt of his own power, or hesitation in speaking his opinions; but a right understanding of the relation between what *he* can do and say and the rest of the world's sayings and doings. All great men not only know their business, but usually know that they know it, and are not only right in their main opinions, but usually know that they are right in them; only, *they do not think much of themselves on that account* [my italics].'

Confucius himself exemplified intellectual humility by refusing to teach subjects of which he lacked sufficient knowledge. Here are two examples:

> Duke Ling of Wei asked Confucius about military formations. Confucius answered, 'I have, indeed, heard something about the use of sacrificial vessels, but I have never studied the matter of commanding troops.' The next day he departed. (15:1)

> Fan Ch'ih asked to be taught how to grow crops. The Master said, 'I am not as good as an old farmer.' He asked to be taught how to grow vegetables. 'I am not as good as an old gardener.' (13:4)

Confucius also showed considerable humility in relation to his young companions. One of them tells us that he was never dogmatic, never conceited: he always refused to 'insist on certainty' or to be egotistical (9:4). He could even defer to excellence when a much younger man surpassed him intellectually:

The Master said to Tzu-kung, 'Who is the better man, you or Hui?'

'How dare I compare myself with Hui? When he is told one thing he understands ten. When I am told one thing I understand only two.'

The Master said, 'You are not as good as he is. Neither of us is as good as he is.' (5:9)

One sure sign of humility in a leader or teacher is the willingness to admit mistakes or errors when they are pointed out. For that recognition and acceptance is the necessary condition for correcting them, thus taking another small step on the long journey to excellence (1:8, 9:25). The only real failure in the book of Confucius is the failure to mend one's ways once an error or mistake becomes clear (14:30).

Confucius himself was willing to accept an implied criticism and respond on the same level. Here are two examples:

When Yen Yüan died, in weeping for him, the Master showed undue sorrow. His followers said, 'You are showing undue sorrow.' 'Am I? Yet if not for him, for whom should I show undue sorrow?' (11:10)

The Master went to Wu Ch'eng. There he heard the sound of stringed instruments and singing. The Master broke into a smile and said, 'Surely you don't need to use an ox-knife to kill a chicken.'

Tzu-yu answered, 'Some time ago I heard it from you, Master, that the gentleman instructed in the Way loves his fellow men and that the small man instructed in the Way is easy to command.'

The Master said, 'My friends, what Yen says is right. My remark a moment ago was only made in jest.' (17:4)

A sense of humour is the natural companion of humility. Lady Violet Bonham-Carter once advised her friend Winston Churchill in a letter that he would be wise to reflect from time to time that even he was just a worm like all the rest of us. (As worms live in *humus*, the earth, the Latin root of humility, they are traditionally a symbol of humility.) When he saw her next, Churchill replied with a smile: 'We are all worms. But I do believe that I am a glow-worm.'

KEY POINTS

- Because of their exaggerated sense of self, arrogant people take upon themselves more power or authority than rightly belongs to them. In contrast, humble people know their limitations: they know what they know, and they know what they do not know; they know what they can do or be, and they know what they cannot do or be. As a consequence, they are not unwilling to heed advice, even when it is unsolicited, or to ask for and accept help.

- Wealth, power and success are breeding grounds for toxic arrogance. 'Power tends to corrupt, and absolute power to corrupt absolutely', wrote the historian Lord Acton in a letter to scholar and ecclesiastic Mandell Creighton in 1887.

- The worst corruption of all for a leader is to believe – and encourage others to believe – that he is more than a person, superhuman or even semi-divine.

- As the Arab proverb goes: 'Arrogance diminishes wisdom'. A humble person, one who lacks all signs of pride both in spirit and in outward show, is walking on a path that leads to practical wisdom.

- Apart from a noticeable lack of egotism, the most common symptoms of humility are an openness

156

to lifelong learning and a willingness to accept
ownership of your own failures, mistakes or
errors.

❧ As you might be told in Ghana: 'Don't expect to be
offered a chair when you visit a place where the
chief himself sits on the floor.'

Sense shines with a double lustre when it is set in
    humility.
An able but humble man is a jewel worth a kingdom.
                                        William Penn

CONCLUSION:
THE PATH TO LEADERSHIP

'Remember that your position does not give you the right to command. It only lays upon you the duty of so living your life that others may receive your orders without being humiliated.'
Dag Hammarskjöld,
Secretary-General of the United Nations

Perhaps while reading this book Heaven has inspired you to become a leader, or, more probably, to become a better one. If so, your feet are already upon the path to leadership. How can Confucius help you further?

The world's tree of knowledge about leadership, which includes the substance of this book, does have a branch or two relating to leadership self-development. As the Bambileke tribes of West Africa say: *You are not born a leader, you become one.*

Often it becomes evident that a boy or girl has some natural potential for leading others during their school years. But potential has to be developed before it can be of any real use.

An early step on the journey towards leadership is to

find the field of human enterprise that most suits your talent – a comprehensive word for your aptitudes, interests and temperament. If you can find this natural fit, you should have no problem later with sustaining your enthusiasm as a leader.

A common pattern in many occupational fields is for a person to spend their first years of work becoming a specialist – what, you remember, Confucius called a 'vessel'. As you progress, you may find that you come to a point where you face a choice – there is a fork in the road. Either you can remain a specialist, or you can broaden out and become a generalist.

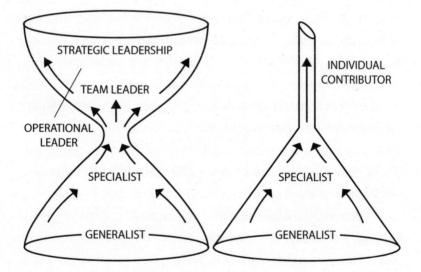

The Hourglass model of career change.

If you decide upon the latter option, doubtless on the advice of others, you are in fact facing the generic role of *leader*, initially as a team leader, then at operational level, and perhaps one day at strategic level. These roles will have different job titles depending on the field that you are in, but, as in a fractal, the underlying or generic role is the same. I outlined that role for you in Chapter 1, so I won't repeat myself here. The key question is: how does one make progress on the path to leadership?

The first principle for making headway is to keep focused on the role of leader and its functional responsibilities, without worrying about your own particular traits or qualities. If you get your functions right, your qualities will look after themselves. As the Spanish say: *What you do, you become.*

In the Western tradition of leadership, the great British prime minister William Gladstone (1809–98) emphasized the importance of doing just that:

> We are to respect our responsibilities, not ourselves.
> We are to respect the duties of which we are capable,
>   not our capabilities simply considered.
> There is to be no complacent self-contemplation,
>   ruminating on self.
> When the self is viewed, it must always be in the
>   most intimate connexion with its purpose.

Your aim, then, is to know what you need to do. That is where the Three Circles model earns its keep, leading to the three broad responsibilities of *achieving the task, building the team* and *developing the individual,* and then onwards to the more specific functions I have listed – such as *planning* or *evaluating.*

The next step is the common-sense one of viewing your strengths in relation to the role: both the generic role of *leader* and the knowledge requirements necessary to fill the position that awaits you. This will help you figure out a set of priorities for self-development that would make Confucius happy. Now get to work on that agenda. *When they call you a reaper, sharpen your scythe.*

In the early stages on the path to leadership, keep going back to the model and the functions (it might help to reread this book, or at least the key points) until it becomes habitual for you to relate principles to practice and practice to principles. For it is when the sparks jump between them that learning happens. Then, as the Chinese say: *The bird carries the wings and the wings carry the bird.*

This habit of reflection – not too little but not too much, as Confucius would advise – will stand you in good stead throughout your career. Think of it as a kind of self-correcting navigation system.

Building on that maritime metaphor, why not think of receiving feedback as a form of taking your bearings?

Feedback is simply information that comes to you about people's reactions – in this case, positive or negative reactions to your performance in the generic role of *leader* as it is embedded in your job.

Don't worry: there will always be plenty of feedback. You shouldn't have to go out of your way to solicit it – just keep your ears and eyes open. Personally, I am against the practice of setting up managerial systems to solicit feedback. In the first place, it sends out the signal of self-centredness; in the second place, there is really no need – it is always there. If you don't know what your partner thinks of you, it's no good sending them a questionnaire.

Remember that all the fragments of feedback that come your way are only personal impressions; no one has the key to your inner self. But the impressions that others form of you are nonetheless facts. Of course, some people will know you better than others and may be more perceptive. Feedback needs to be sifted before it is taken on board, but beware of dismissing the more critical reactions.

The principle is to look out for any pattern in feedback. If bearings fixing your course come from more than one vantage point, then they merit careful attention. As the Hungarian folk saying goes:

> When a man says you are a horse, laugh at him.
> When two men assert you are a horse, give it some
>   thought.

When three men say you are a horse?
You had better go and buy a saddle for yourself.

Going back to Confucius: you should always be on the lookout for a teacher of leadership. And the best teachers – whether they know it or not – are the leaders with whom you come into contact at work. Their example is your copybook. As they say in Uganda: *Leadership is best taught by a leader.*

> The Master said, 'Even when walking in the company of two other men, I am bound to be able to learn from them. The good points of the one I copy; the bad points of the other I correct in myself.' (7:22)

> The Master said, 'When you meet someone better than yourself, turn your thoughts to becoming his equal. When you meet someone not as good as you are, look within and examine your own self.' (4:17)

Paradoxically, as Confucius suggests, you can learn as much if not more from bad examples of leadership as good ones: they shout in your face. So resolve to pluck your lessons from the grey and black geese as well as from snow-white paragons. You will be lucky if you meet one or two of the latter; there is, however, a never-failing supply of poor or abysmal leaders available for your instruction.

It's unwise to continue along the path to leadership and forget the purpose that inspired you to make the arduous journey in the first place. That purpose is service. Therefore, at all stages of your career, put service before the reward you get from it, as Confucius counsels (12:21). Let's hear his voice once more, sounding like a great bronze bell over the world:

> The Master said, 'In serving one's lord, one should approach one's duties with reverence and consider one's pay as of secondary importance.' (15:38)

> Hsien asked about the shameful. The Master said, 'It is shameful to make salary your sole object, irrespective of whether the Way prevails in the state or not.' (14:1)

> The Master said, 'If one is guided by profit in one's actions, one will incur much ill will.' (4:12)

Service according to your talent – in your case, the ability to lead others – is your share of the world's business. The spirit of it is captured in the motto adopted by the

United Kingdom's Chartered Institute of Management on its foundation in 1947, not long after the darkness of war rolled away and there was new hope already dawning in the East: *Ducere est servire* – To lead is to serve.

> Friend, you have read enough.
> If you desire still more,
> then be the odyssey yourself,
> and all that it stands for.
>
> *Angelus Silesius,*
> *seventeenth-century German poet*

APPENDIX:
A BIOGRAPHICAL SKETCH
OF CONFUCIUS

**'Ever since man came into this world, there
has never been one greater than Confucius.'**
Mencius

'Despite his importance in Chinese history, very little is
known about Confucius. The only reliable information
about his life comes from what we can glean from the
Analects and also from the *Tso chuan* (the commentary of
Tso on the *Spring and Autumn Annals*). The book written
by Mencius (*c.* 372–*c.* 289 BCE) is a useful supplement.

Kung Ch'iu, commonly known in the West by his Latin
name Confucius, was born in either 552 or 551 BCE. He
was born in or near Qufu, the capital city of the state of Lu,
which lay in what is now Shandong, the coastal province of
eastern China which occupies the Shandong Peninsula.

Kung was his family name and Chi'iu his given name.
Since it was disrespectful to call a teacher by his given
name, according to Chinese culture, he is known in China
as Kung-tzu, Master Kung, or – in a transliteration system
adopted in the mid-twentieth century – as Kung Zi.

China was without an emperor at this time, though the

idea of empire was far from dead – Confucius himself was a firm believer in it. China was fragmented into states large and small, who often engaged in wars with each other for local dominance. Historians now call it the Spring and Autumn Period, after the title of the main chronicle of the time.

To put the life of Confucius into a wider historical context: he lived at a time when the Persian Empire was in the ascendant, its territory stretching from the borders of India to the shores of the Aegean Sea. In 539 BCE, when Confucius was about twelve, the Persian ruler, Cyrus the Great, allowed the Israelite captives in Babylon to return home and to rebuild the Temple of Jerusalem.

Within the lifetime of Confucius, the Athenian statesman Cleisthenes introduced a democratic constitution for the city – the first in the world. Further afield, Rome had emerged from under the Etruscan shadow and declared itself to be a republic. Tribes such as those of the Celts occupied much of Europe.

At fifteen, I set my heart on learning. At thirty, I found my balance through the rites. At forty, I was free from doubts about myself. At fifty, I understood what Heaven intended me to do. At sixty, I was attuned to what I heard. At seventy, I followed with my heart what my heart desired without overstepping the line. (2:4)

APPENDIX

By tradition, Confucius came from a noble family, but he grew up in humble circumstances. He lost his father when he was three, and his mother died twenty years later. By this time, Confucius had married a young girl called Qi Guan and had fathered their first child, who was called Kung Li.

'I was of humble station when young. That is why I am skilled in many menial things.' (9:6)

Mencius gives us some idea of the way that Confucius made his living by necessity:

Confucius was once a minor official in charge of stores. He said, 'All I have to do is to keep correct records.' He was once put in charge of sheep and cattle. He said, 'All I have to do is to see to it that the sheep and cattle grow up to be strong and healthy.'

According to the *Tso chuan*, Confucius presented himself to the Viscount of T'an, then on a visit to Lu, in order to be instructed about the system in use in the time of Shao Hao of naming offices after birds. At this time Confucius was twenty-seven, and it is likely that he already held some junior post at the Lu court; otherwise, he would hardly have had access to a visiting dignitary.

At some point Confucius became a minister in Lu, probably of the middle rank, in the department of dealing with justice or law and order. He accompanied the Duke of Lu on one successful diplomatic mission to the neighbouring state of Ch'i. But then his career hit the rocks. Lu at this time was dominated by three 'overmighty subjects' – the heads of the three principal noble families, each with their own private feudal army. Apparently Confucius was deeply implicated in an abortive plan to reduce their power by capturing their fortified cities.

Historians tend to link Confucius' loss of office to this event, though the sources give rather less plausible reasons for his departure from the country. In the *Analects*, it is said:

> The men of Ch'i made a present of singing and dancing girls. Ch Huan Tzu accepted them and stayed away from court for three days. Confucius departed. (18:4)

Mencius, however, says:

> Confucius was minister responsible for justice in Lu, but his advice was not followed. He took part in a sacrifice, but, afterwards, was not given a share of the meat of the sacrificial animal. He left the state without waiting to take off his ceremonial cap.
>
> Those who did not understand him thought he acted in this way because of the meat, but those who knew him better realized that he left because Lu failed to observe the proper rites.

For whatever reason, Confucius seems to have gone off on his travels at this juncture. We know that he visited a number of states in his lifetime – Wei, Song, Chen and Cai – some more than once, but we don't know the dates or how long he stayed in each one. If he was looking for employment in the ducal courts, he was unsuccessful, and his advice – solicited or unsolicited – fell on deaf ears.

What happened next is that Confucius – probably in his forties by now – discovered his vocation: to teach the young men of his home state who aspired to become officials and ministers.

Confucius' school – if we can call it that – was open to all young men of promise: neither noble birth nor wealth was a necessary condition for entry.

> The Master said, 'I have never denied instruction to anyone who, of his own accord, has given me so much as a bundle of dried meat as a present.' (7:17)

Like his great Western counterpart Socrates, Confucius charged no fees for teaching leadership: it was the task Heaven had given him. Destiny, not money, was his motive. Thus he exemplified the spirit of disinterested service that he was trying to inculcate into the leader of tomorrow. The words of Lao-tzu apply to Confucius:

> Therefore the sage benefits from them yet exacts no gratitude,

Accomplishes his task yet lays claim to no merit.
Is this not because he does not wish to be considered
    a better man than others? (77:185)

We do not know whereabouts in the vicinity of Qufu
Confucius held his masterclasses. From the *Analects* it
seems as if his own house was in the suburbs. According to
early tradition, there was a Kung family house, modest in
size, which stood in the city near to the Grand Temple of
the Duke of Chou, the legendary founder of the state of
Lu. Confucius revered him above all others as a role model
of what an excellent leader should both do and be.

> The Master said, 'How I have gone downhill! It has
> been such a long time since I dreamt of the Duke of
> Chou.' (7:5)

> Tzu-lu was displeased and said, 'We may have
> nowhere to go but why must we go to Kung-shan?'
>   The Master said, 'The man who summons me
> must have a purpose. If his purpose is to employ me,
> can I not, perhaps, create another Chou in the east?'
> (17:5)

What is certain is that within two years of Confucius'
death in 479 BCE, a house belonging to him which stood
close to the Grand Temple was consecrated as a temple
dedicated to his memory. The house became a shrine where
pilgrims – including eventually some of China's emperors

APPENDIX

– would make their votive offerings at the altars erected
outside.

Wherever his permanent base may have been – the
home where he could play the lute, sing with his friends,
guide the studies of his students and welcome visitors and
guests – Confucius seems to have been a peripatetic teacher.
So much is clear from the recollections of the disciples who
were fortunate enough to accompany him; we have to be
content with the crumbs left under their table. Just being
with him and seeing how he operated must have been a
learning experience in itself.

> Tzu-ch'in asked Tzu-kung, 'When the Master arrives
> in a state, he invariably gets to know about its
> government. Does he seek this information? Or is it
> given to him?'
>
> Tzu-kung said, 'The Master gets it through being
> cordial, good, respectful, frugal and deferential. The
> way the Master seeks it is, perhaps, different from the
> way other men seek it.' (1:10)

> Jan Tzu returned from court. The Master said, 'Why
> so late?' 'There were affairs of state.' The Master said,
> 'They could only have been routine matters. Were
> there affairs of state I would get to hear of them, even
> though I am no longer given any office.' (13:14)

> When the Master went inside the Grand Temple, he
> asked questions about everything. Someone remarked,

'Who said that the son of the man from Tsou [a reference to Confucius' father] understood the rites? When he went inside the Grand Temple, he asked questions about everything.'

The Master, on hearing of this, said, 'The asking of questions is in itself the correct rite.' (3:14; 10:21)

The Master said, 'When housing his great tortoise, Tsang Wen-chung had the capitals of the pillars carved in the shape of hills and the rafterposts painted in a duckweed design. What is one to think of his intelligence?' (5:18)

We may lack the kind of concrete facts about Confucius that historians would desire, but – thanks to the dedication of his inner ring of disciples – we have something infinitely more precious: the *Analects*. John Milton's definition of a good book captures this priceless legacy: 'the lifeblood of a master spirit, embalmed and treasured up to a life beyond life'.

We owe that, as I said, to the devoted disciples who survived Confucius. For them, compiling the *Analects* was clearly a labour of love. Let Yen Yüan speak for them all:

When the Master was under siege in K'uang, Yen Yüan fell behind. The Master said, 'I thought you had met your death.' 'While you, Master, are alive, how would I dare die?' (9:23)

INDEX

best:
  demanding 129, 131
  doing your 38
Bonham-Carter, Lady Violet 155
Botswana 33
Burns, Robert 53

career change, hourglass model of
    160–1
caring for people, importance of
    23, 53–4, 83, 128, 141–2
Catullus 117
Chartered Institute of
    Management 166
Cheshire, Group Captain Leonard
    148
Chi K'ang Tzu 31–2, 35, 36,
    102–3
Chi Tzu-jan 110
Chi Wen Tzu 60
China 1, 2, 3, 38, 134–5, 140
  appointments to administrative
    office, examinations for 44–5
  bad leaders and 38–9
  Han Dynasty and 44–5
  in time of Confucius 167–74
  leader and leadership, meaning
    of words within 10–16
  ministerial resignations within
    110
  modern passion for education
    and technical training 57
  porcelain production 74–5
  Spring and Autumn Period
    168
  Tang Dynasty and 45
  Three Kingdoms period 81n
  wall 27–8
Chinese proverbs 9, 18, 30, 49,

    62, 64, 67, 81, 95, 106, 114,
    133, 137
Ching of Ch'i, Duke 28
Chou, Duke of 145, 172
Chung-kung 93
Churchill, Winston 57, 60, 155
Cicero 42, 44
Clausewitz, Karl von 63
Cleisthenes 39, 168
Collingwood, Admiral 100
common identity 135–40
confidence 30
  honesty and 116
  leading from in front and 30,
    31–48
  self-confidence 63–4
Confucius:
  action, on importance of 51,
    52, 64
  belief in goodness of human
    nature/optimism 37–8, 76,
    133, 142
  biographical sketch of 167–74
  Chinese administrative office
    appointments, influence over
    44–5
  developing the individual, on
    84–5, 88–9, 90, 91, 92–3, 94
  education tailored to
    individual's innate level of
    aptitude, belief in 61
  enthusiasm, on importance of
    100, 101, 102–3, 106
  execution, on importance of 62
  as first great teacher of
    leadership 2, 3, 171–2
  good of the people, stresses
    importance of working for
    53, 54, 140